Chinese Odyssey

Volumes 3 & 4

通向中国

Chinese
Odyssey

Innovative Chinese Courseware

SIMPLIFIED Character Edition

Vols. 3 & 4 • WORKBOOK

Xueying Wang, Li-chuang Chi, and Liping Feng

王学英　　祁立庄　　冯力平

CHENG & TSUI COMPANY Boston

The contents of Chinese Odyssey were developed in part under a grant from the Fund for the Improvement of Postsecondary Education (FIPSE), U.S. Department of Education. However, these contents do not necessarily represent the policy of the Department of Education, and you should not assume endorsement by the Federal Government.

20 19 18 17 16 15 14   3 4 5 6 7 8 9 10

Published by
Cheng & Tsui Company, Inc.
25 West Street
Boston, MA 02111-1213 USA
Fax (617) 426-3669
www.cheng-tsui.com
"Bringing Asia to the World"™

Simplified Character Edition
ISBN-13: 978-0-88727-509-8
ISBN-10: 0-88727-509-5

Printed in the United States of America

Chinese Odyssey includes multimedia products, textbooks, workbooks, and audio products. Visit **www.cheng-tsui.com** for more information on the other components of *Chinese Odyssey*.

Contents

Lesson 32   115

定火车票

Taking the Train

Lesson 33   127

风味小吃

A Taste of China

Lesson 34   139

住旅馆

Staying in a Hotel

Lesson 35   151

锻炼身体

Keep Fit!

Lesson 36   163

我生病了

I Don't Feel Well...

21
请吃饭
Come Eat with Us!

 听力练习(Tīnglì Liànxí)
Listening Exercises

 TASK 1. BINGO

In this section, you will hear various Chinese phrases and sentences. Demonstrate your understanding of them by numbering their English counterparts in the order in which you hear them.

A. Phrases 6 1 8 7 ~ 4 5 3 2

1	congratulations on your new house	1	pour a cup of tea
2	meat and vegetable dishes	2	the best fish
3	everything went smoothly	3	to eat while (the food is) hot ✓
4	the cook's specialty ⌣	4	to be afraid of gaining weight ✓
5	some desserts	5	to use chopsticks ✓
6	(I am) stuffed	6	so skinny ✓
7	toast to friendship	7	not hungry or thirsty ✓
8	after getting a visa	8	to try this kind of chicken ✓

4 1 3 8 7 6 2 5

B. Sentences

9, 3, 6, 1, 2, 8, 4, 7, 5

1 Today I made some of my specialties. ✓

2 I ate lots of fish today. ⌣

3 Now that you've moved into the new house, you should have guests over for dinner. ✓

4 I tried both the meat and the vegetable dishes. ✓

5 The food was so delicious; I ate way too much! ✓

6 Their dining room is so beautiful. ✓

7 He should practice using chopsticks. ⌣

8 These are Mr. Gao's specialties; have some more. ✓

9 Today at their home I ate, drank, and tried desserts. ✓

⌂🖥 TASK 2. SHORT CONVERSATIONS

Listen to the short conversations. Select the correct answer for each question from the choices provided.

1. 好 / 不好
2. 吃了 / 没有吃
3. 男的 / 女的
4. 男的 / 女的

⌂🖥 TASK 3. MONOLOGUE

Listen to the two passages and answer the questions below.

Passage 1

1. What is the woman talking about?

   a) She wants to invite her friends for dinner but does not know how to cook at all.

   b) She wants to invite her friends for dinner but does not know how to cook meat dishes.

   c) She wants to invite her friends for dinner but does not know how to cook vegetable dishes.

   d) None of the above.

2. Which of the following statements is correct?

   a) The woman has already bought everything she needs for the party.

   b) The woman has bought some of what she needs for the party.

   c) The woman has not bought anything for the party yet.

   d) None of the above.

Passage 2

1. What is the man talking about?

   a) He knew exactly what his girlfriend wanted to eat.

   b) He did not know what to order for his girlfriend.

   c) His girlfriend ate a lot.

   d) His girlfriend did not eat much.

2. Why didn't the man's girlfriend eat any dessert?

   a) because she did not like the dessert that was served

   b) because she was full

   c) because the dessert was not served

   d) none of the above

🎧💻 TASK 4. DIALOGUE

Listen to the dialogue and answer the questions below.

1. What is the conversation about?

    a) The man is a good cook.

    b) The woman is a good cook.

    c) Both of them are very good at cooking.

    d) Neither of them can cook.

2. Where does the conversation take place?

    a) at a restaurant

    b) at the woman's home

    c) at the man's place

    d) none of the above

3. Which of the following statements is correct?

    a) The woman has cooked several dishes.

    b) The woman does not eat much.

    c) The woman has enjoyed the food very much.

    d) None of the above.

4. Which of the following is NOT correct?

    a) The man knows how to cook both Chinese and Japanese food.

    b) The women has tried both Chinese and Japanese food.

    c) The man also made some dessert.

    d) The woman likes the man's dessert very much.

口语练习(Kǒuyǔ Liànxí)
Speaking Exercises

🎧💻 TASK 1. SUBSTITUTION

Familiarize yourself with basic sentence patterns by substituting the given phrases into the following sentences.

1. (客人)都(来)了吗?

    还没(来)呢。

他家的人   睡

你的朋友   到

你们   吃

大家   走

2. 我昨天(做的甜点)你(吃)了没有？

(吃)了。

买的茶   喝

借的那本书   看

录的那个故事   听

写的那封信   看

3. 你今天(做)了几(个)(菜)？

两(个)。我还想再(做)一(个)。

买   顶   帽子

借   本   书

看   本   小说

试   条   裤子

4. (吃了饭)，我们再去(签证)，怎么样？

还是(签了证)，再(吃饭)吧。

打(了)电话 上(了)课

写(了)信   喝(了)茶

买(了)东西 跳(了)舞

做(了)作业 收拾(了)房间

5. 你怎么(吃)那么一点儿(甜点)？

我今天想少(吃)一点儿(甜点)，多(吃)一点儿(水果)。

做   菜   饭

喝   咖啡   茶

买   肉   菜

🎧💻 TASK 2. QUICK RESPONSE

The following exercise will challenge your listening and speaking abilities and help you to develop good conversational skills.

A. Answering Questions

Listen to the following questions and provide an answer to each one. If you don't know a word, try to guess its meaning from the context, rather than looking it up. Remember, both speed and accuracy are important!

1. 乔迁之喜是什么意思？

2. 你朋友在你那儿吃饭，你都会说一些什么客气话？

3. 你在你朋友那儿吃饭，你都会说一些什么客气话？

4. 你现在都会说一些什么祝酒词？

B. Asking Questions

Listen to the following statements and follow the hints in the right-hand column to ask a related question for each statement. Try to avoid using the 吗-type question.

	Hints
1. 你做的拿手菜我都尝了。	（没有）
2. 我给他们做了两种甜点。	（几种）
3. 我朋友让我多吃一点儿鱼。	（什么）
4. 因为我刚搬了家，他们要我请大家吃饭。	（为什么）

🎧💻 TASK 3. GUIDED ROLE-PLAYING

Listen to the following dialogues between two native speakers. Then select Role A or Role B and have a dialogue with the computer. After familiarizing yourself with the conversation, construct and record your own dialogue by replacing as many words as possible with related terms. Be creative, but be careful not to disrupt the structure of the conversation!

1. Arrival of a Guest

A: 你今天请我吃什么好菜？这么香！

B: 我做了两个荤菜，两个素菜，都是我的拿手菜。你尝尝。

A: 你做了这么多菜，太辛苦了。

B: 别客气。趁热吃吧。来，你尝一下这个菜。

A: 谢谢。我自己来。你也吃吧。

2. Close to the End of the Dinner

    A: 这个菜你尝了吗？

    B: 尝了，你做的菜好吃极了。

    A: 慢慢吃，一会儿还要上甜点呢。

    B: 我吃得太饱了。来，干一杯。为我们的友谊干杯。

    A: 也为你的新工作干杯。

    B: 干杯，干杯。

TASK 4. PICTURE DESCRIPTION

Describe the pictures below using the grammar and the vocabulary you learned in this lesson. Use your imagination!

读写练习(Dú Xiě Liànxí)
Reading/Writing Exercises

 TASK 1. SHORT STORY

Read the story and answer the questions that follow.

乔迁之喜

阿乐那天下午回家取了阿笑家房子的图纸以后，就买了跟阿笑家一样的房子。很快他就搬了家。搬家是一件高兴的事，所以搬家也叫乔迁之喜。中国人常常请朋友在新家吃饭，庆祝乔迁之喜。所以阿乐买了房子以后，请了阿笑和阿笑太太周末来家里吃饭。

阿乐做了很多他的拿手菜，有荤的也有素的。阿乐还买了一些好酒，请阿笑喝。阿笑非常高兴，又吃菜，又喝酒。两个小时以后阿笑的太太怕阿笑喝酒喝得太多，就找了个借口跟阿笑说：咱们回家吧，我吃得太饱了。想回家休息休息。阿笑说：吃饱了饭,不能马上走。你就在这儿休息休息吧。又过了一个小时，阿笑还在喝酒。阿笑太太不想让阿笑再喝酒，就说：我现在不那么饱了，我们走吧。阿笑跟他太太说：那你就再吃一点儿，不要客气。我们在朋友家吃饭，怎么能没吃饱就走呢？

Supplementary Vocabulary

1. 跟…一样	gēn…yīyàng	*phr.*	the same as…
2. 周末	zhōumò	*n.*	weekend
3. 又…又	yòu… yòu	*adv.*	again
4. 过	guò	*v.*	to pass
5. 小时	xiǎoshí	*n.*	hour
6. 借口	jièkǒu	*n.*	excuse

Questions

1. 中国人搬家以后要请朋友在哪儿吃饭？

   a) 在朋友家

   b) 在饭馆

   c) 在自己家

   d) a, b, c 都不对

2. 阿笑为什么不想回家？

   a) 因为他还想喝酒。

   b) 因为他太太还没吃饱。

   c) 因为他太太吃得太饱了。

   d) a, b, c 都不对。

3. 阿笑的太太为什么想回家？

   a) 因为她不想喝酒。

   b) 因为阿笑喝酒喝得太多了。

   c) 因为阿乐的饭不好吃。

   d) a, b, c 都不对。

4. 下面哪句话是对的？

   a) 阿笑刚搬了家，非常高兴。

   b) 阿笑的太太很怕阿笑。

   c) 阿乐很会做饭。

   d) a, b, c 都对。

TASK 2. AUTHENTIC MATERIAL

In this section, you will be exposed to some authentic materials that people use in China. Read the following letter of invitation from someone who just moved to a new place, and answer the questions below.

Questions

1. 这是一封什么样的信？
2. 他们为什么开晚会？
3. 他们什么时候开晚会？
4. 他们请谁来参加晚会？

TASK 3. SENTENCE CONSTRUCTION

Create your own questions using the phrases in the "Question" rows, and then answer the questions using the words in the "Response" rows.

1. Ask your friend if he/she wants to go with you to the embassy after breakfast tomorrow to get a visa.

    Question: 早饭，签证

    Response: 好啊，也还没有

2. Ask your friend what dish he/she brought to the party yesterday.

    Question: 晚会，带

    Response: 甜点，喜欢

3. Ask your friend if he/she bought the food he/she was told to buy yesterday.

    Question: 菜，买

    Response: 还没有，一会儿去

4. Ask your friend what he/she ate at the party.

    Question: 在他们家，好菜

    Response: 做的，拿手菜

 TASK 4. E-MAIL

You have had a fantastic weekend, and you want to tell your friend all about it. Write your friend an e-mail and tell him/her about all the things you did over the weekend. Did you sleep late? After you got out of bed, what did you do? Did you have a big breakfast, brunch, or dinner? What did you do in the afternoon? Did you visit your friends or relatives? Did anyone visit you? Was there anything you were supposed to do but didn't? Don't forget to use 了!

22

办签证
How Do I Get a Visa?

听力练习(Tīnglì Liànxí)
Listening Exercises

🎧💻 TASK 1. BINGO

In this section, you will hear various Chinese phrases and sentences. Demonstrate your understanding of them by numbering their English counterparts in the order in which you hear them.

A. Phrases

15, 3, 6, 5, 7, 12, 13, 11, 4, 1, 16, 8, 9, 10, , 2, 14

1 don't make corrections

2 don't worry

3 admissions letter from a university

4 a photo

5 Chinese Embassy

6 to write very clearly

7 should be very careful

8 American passport

9 two misspelled words

10 to stand in line here

11 to fill in your nationality

12 a tourist visa

13 to write it again

14 employee/staff

15 to forget to bring American dollars

16 very close to school

B. Sentences

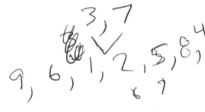

3, 7 9, 6, 1, 2, 5, 8, 4

✓1 She went to the Embassy yesterday and got the visa to China.

✓2 Excuse me, can you give me another form? I need to fill it out again.

✓3 You forgot to sign. Please sign your name here.

✓4 He forgot to bring his passport today, so he has to go there again tomorrow.

✓5 Last night I looked for you twice, but you were not there. Where did you go?

✓6 Did my letter of admission arrive?

✓7 Is the embassy far from your home?

✓8 How about picking up the photos after class tomorrow?

✓9 Don't worry. He does not make mistakes when he handles affairs.

🎧💻 TASK 2. SHORT CONVERSATIONS

Listen to the short conversations. Select the correct answer for each question from the choices provided.

1. 细心 /(不细心)
2. 有 /(没有)
3. (有)/ 没有
4. (是 / 不是)
5. 知道 /(不知道)

🎧💻 TASK 3. MONOLOGUE

Listen to the two passages and answer the questions below.

Passage 1

1. What is this passage about?

   a) The woman just got her passport.

   b) The woman just got her visa.

   c) The woman is going to study abroad.

   d) None of the above.

2. Which of the following statements is NOT correct?

   a) The woman likes Chinese literature.

   b) The woman has never been to the Chinese Embassy.

   c) The woman has not received her visa yet.

   d) The woman has not received her passport yet.

Passage 2

1. What is this passage about?

   a) The speaker is very proud of his friend's Chinese language skills.

   b) The speaker's friend is proud of the speaker's Chinese language skills.

   c) The speaker's friend lacks attention to detail.

   d) The speaker lacks attention to detail.

2. Which of the following statements is correct?

    a) The speaker's friend filled out a visa application form very carefully.

    b) The speaker filled out a visa application form very carefully.

    c) The speaker's friend filled out a visa application form very carelessly.

    d) The speaker filled out a visa application form very carelessly.

🎧💻 TASK 4. DIALOGUE

Listen to the dialogue and answer the questions below.

1. What is the conversation about?

    a) where the two speakers are going to school

    b) how well the two speakers like their photos

    c) how frequently the two speakers get together

    d) none of the above

2. Where does the conversation take place?

    a) at school

    b) on the street

    c) at the embassy

    d) none of the above

3. Which of the following is correct?

    a) The man is going to study in China.

    b) The woman is going to study in China.

    c) Both the man and the woman are going to study in China.

    d) None of the above.

4. Which of the following statements is NOT correct?

    a) The man and the woman have never been to Chinese Embassy before.

    b) This is the third time the man has been to the Chinese Embassy.

    c) This is the first time the woman has been to the Chinese Embassy.

    d) The man and the woman have never met before.

口语练习(Kǒuyǔ Liànxí)
Speaking Exercises

🎧📖 TASK 1. SUBSTITUTION

Familiarize yourself with basic sentence patterns by substituting the given phrases into the following sentences.

1. 你这个星期去(大使馆)了吗?

   我去了(两)次了!

商店买东西	三
饭馆吃饭	四
图书馆借书	五
宿舍找他	六

2. 你昨天下午去哪儿了?

   昨天我(吃了中午饭)就(去取照片)了。

看了电影	跟朋友去跳舞
帮朋友搬了家	回家休息
下了课	回宿舍
开了会	去上课

3. (去中国上学的申请表)你(填)了没有?

   (填)了。我都(填)了两遍了。你呢?

老师给的中文作业	做
申请工作的个人简历	写
我写的小说	看
今天学的中文字	练习

4. 你准备什么时候（去办签证）？

   急什么？现在离（去中国）还有两个星期呢。

复习课文和语法	考试
去买裙子	舞会
订做生日蛋糕	他的生日
搬家	修房子

5. 你（取了照片）了吗？

   还没呢。（商店）离我宿舍很近。一会儿去。

借了书	图书馆
吃了饭	食堂
去了他工作的地方	他的公司
问了问题	老师的办公室

🎧💻 TASK 2. QUICK RESPONSE

The following exercise will challenge your listening and speaking abilities and help you to develop good conversational skills.

A. Answering Questions

Listen to the following questions and provide an answer to each one. If you don't know a word, try to guess its meaning from the context, rather than looking it up. Remember, both speed and accuracy are important!

1. 办学生签证需要带什么东西？

2. 你准备去中国，你想办什么签证？为什么？

3. 昨天下了课，你做什么了？

4. 你家离什么地方近，离什么地方远？

B. Asking Questions

Listen to the following statements and follow the hints in the right-hand column to ask a related question for each statement. Try to avoid using the 吗-type question.

	Hints
1. 我还没有签名呢。	（了没有）
2. 我今天办了签证就回学校了。	（哪儿）
3. 我下个星期去大使馆办签证。	（什么时候）
4. 大使馆离我们学校太远了。	（为什么没）

🎧📓 TASK 3. GUIDED ROLE-PLAYING

Listen to the following dialogues between two native speakers. Then select Role A or Role B and have a dialogue with the computer. After familiarizing yourself with the conversation, construct and record your own dialogue by replacing as many words as possible with related terms. Be creative, but be careful not to disrupt the structure of the conversation!

1. What Visa Are You Applying For?

   A: 今天早上我给你打了几个电话，你都不在。你去哪儿了？

   B: 我去中国大使馆办签证了。明天还要再去一次。

   A: 你为什么要去这么多次？

   B: 我忘了带照片了。

   A: 你去使馆办什么签证？学生签证，旅游签证，还是工作签证？

   B: 旅游签证。

2. What Do I Need for My Visa Application?

   A: 现在离我们去中国还有一个月。你的签证办了吗？

   B: 我还没有办。你呢？

   A: 大使馆离我家很近。我上个月就办了签证了。

   B: 办签证的时候，应该带什么东西？

   A: 要带护照，两张照片，学校录取通知书和美金。

   B: 要不要填表？

   A: 当然要填表啦。你要填签证申请表。

TASK 4. PICTURE DESCRIPTION

Describe the pictures below using the grammar and the vocabulary you learned in this lesson. Use your imagination!

 读写练习(Dú Xiě Liànxí)
Reading/Writing Exercises

TASK 1. CHENGYU STORY

In this section, you will be exposed to a Chinese 成语故事 (chéngyǔ gùshi). A 成语 is usually a four-character phrase in Chinese. It is a humorous way of teaching people a set of morals or a piece of wisdom. A 成语故事 is a story that describes where the 成语 comes from. Read the story below and answer the following questions.

天衣无缝

很久很久以前，有一个做衣服的人，他的名字叫阿全。他每天都做衣服，大家都说他的衣服做得很漂亮。可是他自己总是觉得自己做的衣服有缺陷，但是他不知道什么衣服是没有缺陷的。

一天晚上，阿全在自己的院子里做衣服。一个穿了一件白衣服的姑娘从天上飞了下来。那个姑娘对阿全说："我是天上的织女，我今天到你这儿来，是让你看看我们天上织女做的衣服。"阿全非常高兴，他看了几遍那个织女穿的衣服。他想这个姑娘的衣服真的非常漂亮，这可能就是我想做的那种没有缺陷的衣服吧。他想了想，又看了一遍织女的衣服，他发现这个织女的衣服，没有一点儿用针线缝的地方。他很好奇，就问织女她的衣服是怎么做的？为什么没有用针线缝的地方？织女回答说："我的衣服是天衣，不是用针线缝的。"所以，大家以后就用天衣无缝来描述没有缺陷的东西。

Supplementary Vocabulary

1. 天衣无缝	tiānyī wúfèng	phr.	flawless
天		n.	sky, the heavens
衣		n.	clothing
无		adv.	no, have not
缝		n.	stitch
2. 很久	hěn jiǔ	phr.	long time
3. 缺陷	quēxiàn	n.	flaw, defect
4. 姑娘	gūniang	n.	girl
5. 天上	tiānshàng	phr.	the sky, in the sky
6. 飞了下来	fēi le xiàlai	phr.	flying/floating down
7. 织女	zhīnǚ	phr.	knitting/weaving woman from heaven
8. 发现	fāxiàn	v.	to discover
9. 针线	zhēnxiàn	n.	needle and thread, needlework

10. 缝	féng	*v.*	to sew
11. 描述	miáoshù	*v.*	to describe

Questions

1. 那个做衣服的人觉得自己做的衣服是最好的。 True/False
2. 那个做衣服的人做的衣服跟天上的衣服一样好看。 True/False
3. 织女的衣服十全十美是因为天衣只要用针线缝一遍。 True/False
4. 办事没有错误就是天衣无缝。 True/False

TASK 2. AUTHENTIC MATERIAL

In this section, you will be exposed to some authentic materials that people use in China. Read the following form and answer the questions below.

中华人民共和国签证申请表 **(Q1)**

（此表不适用于香港特区）

请用大写字母填写

请认真阅读背面的注意事项

1. 中文姓名	2. 曾用名	3. 性别 □ 男 □ 女	照片 2"×2"
4. 外文姓名			
5. 出生日期: 年 月 日	6. 出生地		
7. 国籍	8. 曾有何国籍		
9. 职业	工作单位电话 ( ) –		
工作单位			
10. 家庭住址	电话 ( ) –		
11. 护照种类: 普通 □ 外交 □ 公务 (官员) □ 其他证件(名称) □			
护照有效期: 年 月 日	发照机关:	护照号码:	
12. 申请赴中国事由			
13. 前往中国地点			
14. 计划入境的次数 □ 一次 □ 二次 □ 多次	15. 预计入境的日期 ① 年 月 日 ② 年 月 日		
16. 预计每次在中国停留天数	① 天 ② 天		
17. 计划取证件日期 □ 正常(4个工作日) □ 加急(2-3个工作日) □ 特急(当天)			
18. 邀请单位名称或邀请人姓名、地址、电话			
19. 你是否申请过赴华签证	□ 是 □ 否		
20. 你是否被拒绝过赴华签证 被拒绝时间.地点	□ 是 □ 否		
我谨声明，我已如实和完整地填写了上述内容，并对所填写内容负责 日期: 年 月 日 申请人签名			

此表可复印使用

Questions

1. 谁应该填写这张表？
2. 哪些号码的格子是问填表人的个人问题？
3. 哪一个格子是问"护照"的问题？
4. 你要去两次中国，应该填哪一个格子？

 ## TASK 3. SENTENCE CONSTRUCTION

Create your own questions using the phrases in the "Question" rows, and then answer the questions using the words in the "Response" rows.

1. Suggest that you and your friend go and pick up your passports together. However, your friend has already picked up his passport.

   Question: 下了课，取护照

   Response: 离…很近，取了

2. Ask your friend if he or she has applied for a visa to China. He or she has.

   Question: 签证，办

   Response: 护照以后，签证

3. After being told that the form you filled out has a few misspellings, you want to fill out another form.

   Question: 错别字，细心

   Response: 再，一遍

4. Ask your friend why he/she has to make another trip to the embassy.

   Question: 一次，还要去

   Response: 去的时候，忘了

TASK 4. E-MAIL

You just came back from a trip abroad and want to tell your friend all about it. E-mail him/her and explain the preparations you made for the trip. Where did you go? What did you do there? Did you need a visa? What kind? Did you finally get it? How many times did you have to go to the embassy? Why? Be sure to use the grammar and vocabulary you learned in this lesson.

23
送人
Seeing Someone Off

 听力练习 (Tīnglì Liànxí)
Listening Exercises

 TASK 1. BINGO

In this section, you will hear various Chinese phrases and sentences. Demonstrate your understanding of them by numbering their English counterparts in the order in which you hear them.

A. Phrases

1 to leave America

3 the entrance

5 to check in two pieces of luggage

7 to have a pleasant trip

9 on-time departure

11 directly to Beijing

13 security checkpoint

15 to drop somebody off at the airport

2 to buy airplane tickets

4 to go through procedures (paperwork)

6 computer screen

8 to pick up a boarding pass

10 to change a flight

12 airport waiting room

14 to take motion sickness pills

16 aisle seat

10, 7, 1, 6, 5, 16, 8,
2, 14, 3, 4, 15, 11, 12
13, 9

B. Sentences

1 The flight is about to leave. Please prepare to board the airplane.

2 You just went to check the departure time. Why are you going again?

3 We're going to board at 9:30.

4 She is very sad because her friends are leaving America soon.

5 If the flight is delayed, we can go and get another cup of coffee.

6 Can the luggage be sent directly to Beijing?

7 Do you have any window seats (available)?

8 Let's ask for an aisle seat.

9 Last time he flew, he did not check in any luggage; this time he did not either.

6, 3, 9, 1, 4, 8, 2, 5, 7

21

🎧💻 TASK 2. SHORT CONVERSATIONS

Listen to the short conversations. Select the correct answer for each question from the choices provided.

1. 在飞机上 / 在飞机场
2. 在飞机上 / 在飞机场
3. 男的 / 女的
4. 上了 / 没有上
5. 好了 / 没有

🎧💻 TASK 3. MONOLOGUE

Listen to the two passages and answer the questions below.

Passage 1

1. What is this passage about?

    a) The speaker is not ready for her trip abroad.

    b) The speaker is unwilling to leave her friend.

    c) The speaker needs to buy some medicine for her trip.

    d) None of the above.

2. Which of the following statements is correct?

    a) The speaker's flight is delayed.

    b) The speaker finished packing several days ago.

    c) The speaker has motion sickness.

    d) None of the above.

Passage 2

1. What is this passage about?

    a) Both the speaker and his friend are going to China.

    b) The speaker's friend is taking the speaker to the airport.

    c) The speaker is taking his friend to the airport.

    d) None of the above.

2.   Where is the man?

   a) He is on his way to the airport.

   b) He is at the airport.

   c) He is on the airplane.

   d) None of the above.

🎧💻 TASK 4. DIALOGUE

Listen to the dialogue and answer the questions below.

1.   What is this conversation about?

   a) The woman is leaving for China.

   b) The man is leaving for China.

   c) Both of the speakers are leaving for China.

   d) Neither of the speakers is leaving for China.

2.   Where does the conversation take place?

   a) on the way to the airport

   b) on the airplane

   c) at the airport

   d) none of the above

3.   Whose feelings are best described below?

   a) The woman is very sad.

   b) The man is very sad.

   c) Both of them are very sad.

   d) Neither of them is very sad.

4.   Which of the following statements is correct?

   a) The flight is delayed.

   b) The flight is on time.

   c) Neither speaker knows whether the flight is on time or delayed.

   d) None of the above.

口语练习(Kǒuyǔ Liànxí)
Speaking Exercises

🎧💻 TASK 1. SUBSTITUTION

Familiarize yourself with basic sentence patterns by substituting the given phrases into the following sentences.

1. 昨天他(去机场送了人)，今天他又要(去机场送人)了。

   请了客   请客
   跳了舞   跳舞
   考了试   考试
   看了电影   看电影

2. 我中午(听了听新闻)。没意思。晚上不想再(听)了。

   看了看电视   看
   聊了聊天   聊
   看了看报   看
   写了写信   写

3. 再不(去买机票)，我就(不去北京)了。

   去吃饭   饿死
   去买新衣服   不去听音乐会
   去食堂   自己做饭
   搬家   没地方住

4. (飞机)是不是就要(起飞)了？

   不，还要等一会儿呢。

   电影   开始
   他们   睡觉

商店　　开门

晚饭　　做好

5. A: 飞机(要)起飞了，我们准备登机吧。

　　B: 再见了，美国！我们就要去(北京)了。

　　　　快要　　　日本

　　　　就要　　　法国

　　　　马上要　　英国

　　　　五点就要　德国

6. A: 你还有(半个小时)就要离开这儿了，我很难过。

　　B: 你别难过了。我们再过(几个星期)，又能见面了。

　　　　两个小时　二十天

　　　　两天　　　两个星期

　　　　两个星期　三个月

　　　　两个月　　两年

🎧💻 TASK 2. QUICK RESPONSE

The following exercise will challenge your listening and speaking abilities and help you to develop good conversational skills.

A. Answering Questions

Listen to the following questions and provide an answer to each one. If you don't know a word, try to guess its meaning from the context, rather than looking it up. Remember, both speed and accuracy are important!

1. 登机以前，应该办哪些手续？

2. 在飞机上，你喜欢坐什么座位？为什么？

3. 你怎么能知道飞机是不是准时起飞？

4. 你的朋友要登机了，你应该跟他说什么？

B. Asking Questions

Listen to the following statements and follow the hints in the right-hand column to ask a related question for each statement. Try to avoid using the 吗-type question.

	Hints
1. 我要托运四件行李。	（几件）
2. 我马上就吃晕机药。	（怎么又）
3. 我想看看飞机是不是准时起飞。	（为什么又）
4. 没问题，行李都能直接到北京。	（能不能）

🎧💻 TASK 3. GUIDED ROLE-PLAYING

Listen to the following dialogues between two native speakers. Then select Role A or Role B and have a dialogue with the computer. After familiarizing yourself with the conversation, construct and record your own dialogue by replacing as many words as possible with related terms. Be creative, but be careful not to disrupt the structure of the conversation!

1. Checking in at the Airport

   A: 您好，我去中国北京。这是我的护照和机票。

   B: 托运几件行李？

   A: 两件。我有的时候晕机，请你查一查有没有靠前边的座位？

   B: 请稍等。

   A: 麻烦你再看一看有没有靠走道的座位？

   B: 有。这是您的登机牌，请到12号登机口登机。祝您旅途愉快。

2. Seeing Someone off at the Airport

   A: 你的飞机九点就要起飞了。我真不想让你走。

   B: 别难过了。我也不想离开你。

   A: 旅途很辛苦，你不要太累了。

   B: 放心吧。你回家吧。我们过几个星期，又要见面了。

   A: 好吧。到了以后，别忘了给我打电话。祝你一路平安。

TASK 4. PICTURE DESCRIPTION

Describe the pictures below using the grammar and the vocabulary you learned in this lesson. Use your imagination!

 读写练习(Dú Xiě Liànxí)
Reading/Writing Exercises

 TASK 1. SHORT STORY

Read the story and answer the questions that follow.

我们应该再早一点来

阿乐代表他的电脑公司去中国做生意。阿笑到飞机场去送他。到了机场以后，阿笑去停车，阿乐自己去托运行李，取登机牌。阿乐因为晕机，跟工作人员要了一个靠前面的座位，一切都很顺利。一会儿阿笑停了车，来找阿乐。阿乐对阿笑说："我刚才在等你的时候，看了一下离港的屏幕，飞机将会在上午十点整准时起飞，现在时间还早，我在椅子上睡一会儿，再去登机口。"阿笑也觉得阿乐是应该睡一会儿，因为阿乐今天起床起得非常早。

十点以后，阿笑对阿乐说：阿乐，你醒一醒，你的飞机刚刚起飞了。阿乐很难过，他对阿笑说：咱们应该再早一点来机场就好了。

Supplementary Vocabulary

| 代表 | dàibiǎo | v. | to represent, to stand for, on behalf of |
| 醒一醒 | xǐng yi xǐng | v. phr. | to wake up |

Questions

1. 谁要去中国？

   a) 阿乐要去中国。

   b) 阿笑要去中国。

   c) 阿乐和阿笑都要去中国。

   d) 阿乐和阿笑都不去中国。

2. 飞机起飞了以后，谁在飞机上？

   a) 阿乐在飞机上。

   b) 阿笑在飞机上。

   c) 阿乐和阿笑都在飞机上。

   d) 阿乐和阿笑都不在飞机上。

3. 阿乐和阿笑什么时候到飞机场的？

   a) 飞机快要起飞的时候

   b) 离飞机起飞还有很长时间。

   c) 飞机起飞以后

   d) a, b, c 都不对。

4. 下面哪个句子是对的？

　　a) 阿乐和阿笑应该再早一点来机场。

　　b) 阿乐不应该去托运行李。

　　c) 阿乐不应该睡觉。

　　d) a, b, c 都不对。

 ## TASK 2. AUTHENTIC MATERIAL

In this section, you will be exposed to some authentic materials that people use in China. Look at the map of Capital International Airport and answer the following questions.

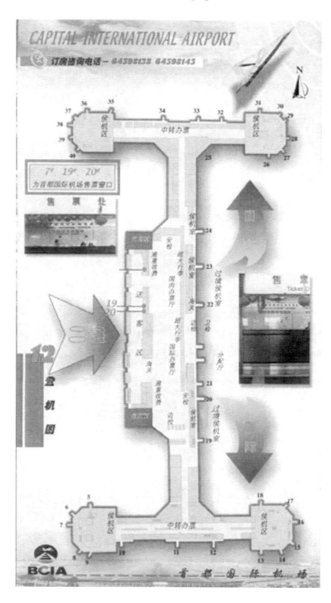

Questions

1. 这个飞机场有几个海关？几个安全检查口？
2. 飞机场有几个窗口可以买机票？
3. 5号到18号是什么？
4. 过境的候机室都多少号？

 TASK 3. SENTENCE CONSTRUCTION

Create your own sentences using the phrases in the "Statement" rows, and then respond using the words in the "Response" rows.

1. Warn your friend about the consequences of his or her not taking motion sickness medicine.

    Statement: 再不，就又要

    Response: 飞机场，再吃

2. Tell your friend how sad you feel about him or her leaving.

    Statement: 快要，难过

    Response: 别，今年十二月

3. Ask if there are any aisle seats left.

    Statement: 还有，靠

    Response: 只有，窗口

4. Ask why your friend keeps going to check the departure time.

    Statement: 又去，到港—离港

    Response: 再看看，准时起飞

 TASK 4. E-MAIL

You have just arrived in a new city and are feeling a little homesick when you receive an instant message from a friend. Reply to the message, explaining your mood and describing the scene when you left home. Who drove you to the airport (train station, etc.)? Were you sad to leave? Did you forget to pack anything? Have you phoned anyone since arriving? Were they worried about you? Remember that in narration, you don't have to use 了 all over the place! But do use the vocabulary and grammar from the lesson.

24
到达北京机场
We Made It!

 听力练习 (Tīnglì Liànxí)
Listening Exercises

 TASK 1. BINGO

In this section, you will hear various Chinese phrases and sentences. Demonstrate your understanding of them by numbering their English counterparts in the order in which you hear them.

A. Phrases

1 to provide help

3 to start descending

5 to distribute the customs entry cards

7 finally arrived

9 first time

11 to fill out a customs declaration form

13 too excited

15 two or three flight attendants

2 to complete a task

4 to talk to someone on the phone

6 on the sign

8 more than twenty hours

10 to listen carefully

12 already one hour and thirty minutes

14 on top of the luggage shelf

16 a few hundred passengers

10 6 1 4 7 12

13 2 5 9 14 16

15 11 8 3

B. Sentences

It took him more than an hour to fill out a customs declaration form.

After communicating via e-mail for more than two years, we finally met in person.

He did not get up until he had slept for more than ten hours yesterday.

They already talked to each other on the phone several times today.

It is said that this is his first time traveling to the United States.

How long have you lived in Beijing?

He is very excited. In just two more hours, the airplane will arrive in America.

In about ten minutes we will arrive in Beijing, China.

Please do your paperwork for going through customs.

🎧💻 TASK 2. SHORT CONVERSATIONS

Listen to the short conversations. Select the correct answer for each question from the choices provided.

1. 办了／没办
2. 是／不是
3. 见了／没见
4. 发完了／没发完
5. 长／不长
6. 是／不是

🎧💻 TASK 3. MONOLOGUE

Listen to the two passages and answer the questions below.

Passage 1

1. What is the man talking about?

   a) He left the U.S. three months ago.

   b) He was very busy when he was in Beijing.

   c) He needs some good sleep.

   d) None of the above.

2. Where is the man?

   a) He is on his way back from Beijing to the U.S.

   b) He is on his way to Beijing from the U.S.

   c) He is already in Beijing.

   d) He is back in the U.S.

Passage 2

1. What is this woman talking about?

   a) The woman is satisfied with her Chinese language skills.

   b) The woman is not satisfied with her Chinese language skills.

   c) The woman is very satisfied with the form she filled out.

   d) None of the above.

2. Which one of the following is NOT correct?

    a) The woman takes a long time to fill out the form.

    b) It is very easy for the woman to fill out the form.

    c) The woman completes the form more than once.

    d) The form the woman fills out has many mistakes on it.

🎧 TASK 4. DIALOGUE

Listen to the dialogue and answer the questions below.

1. What does the woman not want the man to do?

    a) to eat

    b) to fill out the forms

    c) to sleep

    d) none of the above

2. What does the man forget to do?

    a) to eat

    b) to fill out the forms

    c) to sleep

    d) none of the above

3. When does this conversation take place?

    a) before the airplane takes off

    b) during the flight

    c) after the airplane has landed

    d) none of the above

4. How much time is left before the airplane arrives at the Beijing airport?

    a) 1 hour

    b) 50 minutes

    c) 30 minutes

    d) 15 minutes

口语练习 (Kǒuyǔ Liànxí)

Speaking Exercises

 TASK 1. SUBSTITUTION

Familiarize yourself with basic sentence patterns by substituting the given phrases into the following sentences.

1. 你(睡觉)(睡)了多久?

   我(睡)了(三个半小时)。

做生意	做	两年半
搞电脑	搞	四个半星期
学唱歌	学	三天多
谈对象	谈	五个半月

2. 你学了多久的(中文)了?

   我学了(一)年多的(中文)了。

文学	三
外语	四
数学	五
电脑	六

3. 你在(中国)住了多长时间?

   我住了(二十多年)。

英国	两年多
日本	两个多月
法国	十几年
德国	几天

4. 你(填)(表)了吗？

  我正在(填)，我已经(填)了十几分钟了。

  收拾　　　　　房间

  看　　　　　电视新闻

  读　　　　　课文

  看　　　　　今天的报

5. 从北京到上海(飞机要飞)多长时间？

  要(飞)(好几)个小时。

  开车要开　　　　　　　开　　二十几

  走路要走　　　　　　　走　　几百

  骑(qí, ride)车要骑　　　骑　　一百多

6. 我们(填表填)了(一、两)个小时才完成任务。

  他们(十几分钟)就完成任务了。

  搬家搬　　　　七、八　　半小时

  修椅子修　　　四、五　　二十几分钟

  做作业做　　　两、三　　几分钟

  写个人简历写　三、四　　五分钟

🎧💻 TASK 2. QUICK RESPONSE

The following exercise will challenge your listening and speaking abilities and help you to develop good conversational skills.

A. Answering Questions

Listen to the following questions and provide an answer to each one. If you don't know a word, try to guess its meaning from the context, rather than looking it up. Remember, both speed and accuracy are important!

1. 你学中文学了几年了？

2. 你每天睡几个小时的觉？

3. 你每个星期看多长时间的电视？

4. 你和你的好朋友认识了多久了？

B. Asking Questions

Listen to the following statements and follow the hints in the right-hand column to ask a related question for each statement. Try to avoid using the 吗-type question.

		Hints
1.	飞机晚了一个多小时。	（几个）
2.	我休息了半个多小时。	（多久）
3.	我们还有两、三个小时就到北京了。	（多长时间）
4.	我们填表填了好几遍。	（多少）

💻 TASK 3. GUIDED ROLE-PLAYING

Listen to the following dialogues between two native speakers. Then select Role A or Role B and have a dialogue with the computer. After familiarizing yourself with the conversation, construct and record your own dialogue by replacing as many words as possible with related terms. Be creative, but be careful not to disrupt the structure of the conversation!

1. Arriving at the Airport

   A: 飞机还有多久才能到达北京机场呢？

   B: 还有一个多小时吧。你看飞机现在已经开始下降了。

   A: 你知道不知道办入关手续要用多长时间？

   B: 真正办手续只要几分钟。但是要排队。

   A: 这是我第一次填入关卡和入境申报表，您帮我看看我填的对不对，好吗？

   B: 没问题。

2. Picking a Friend up Late at the Airport

   A: 谢谢你来机场接我们。

   B: 别客气。你们飞机晚点了，飞了二十多个小时，累了吧。

   A: 我睡了十几个小时，一点儿也不累。但是让你等了这么长时间。真对不起。

   B: 别客气。你们路上顺利吗？多长时间没吃饭了？

   A: 路上挺顺利。只是好几个小时没吃饭了。现在有一点儿饿了。

   B: 那我们取了行李，我就请你去吃饭。

TASK 4. PICTURE DESCRIPTION

Describe the pictures below using the grammar and the vocabulary you learned in this lesson. Use your imagination!

读写练习(Dú Xiě Liànxí)
Reading/Writing Exercises

 TASK 1. SHORT STORY

Read the story and answer the True/False questions that follow.

阿乐接人

阿乐公司的陈老板很厉害，大家都怕他，但是陈老板很怕他太太。一天下午陈老板的太太旅游累了，想回家休息休息，要陈老板去机场接他。但是陈老板下午有事不能去接她，就叫阿乐代表他去机场接他太太。阿乐用了四十五分钟的时间写了一个大牌子"阿乐代表《中文软件公司》陈老板来机场接他的太太"。牌子写完了以后，阿乐很得意，觉得自己很聪明。那天下午阿乐开了一个小时的车，就到了机场。过了十几分钟，飞机到了。有一位三十几岁的漂亮女士问阿乐："我可不可以坐你的车去你的公司见陈老板？"阿乐总是喜欢帮助漂亮女人，他说："当然可以，我就是来接你的，快上车吧！"阿乐马上帮她拿行李。阿乐装完车，正要走的时候，有一位四十多岁的丑女士走了过来。她对阿乐说："这是中文软件公司的车吗？陈老板正在公司等我，你是来接我的吗？"阿乐很不耐烦，对她说："你要去中文软件公司，就去那边坐出租车。这位漂亮女士才是我要接的人，再见！"阿乐到达公司的时候，陈老板已经在公司外边等了二十多分钟了。这位漂亮女士看见陈老板，非常高兴，她说："陈老板，您怎么还来接我，我跟你的面试是明天，对吗？"陈老板看车里没有他太太，他很着急，问阿乐："我的太太呢？"

Supplementary Vocabulary

1. 得意	déyì	*adj.*	be pleased with oneself, complacent
2. 女士	nǚshì	*n.*	lady
3. 拿	ná	*v.*	to hold, to take

4. 装   zhuāng   *v.*   to load

5. 不耐烦   bú nàifán   *adj.*   impatient

Questions

1. 阿乐没做准备就去机场接陈老板的太太了。   True/False

2. 阿乐到了机场以后，很快就完成了陈老板给他的任务。   True/False

3. 陈老板在公司外边见了他太太以后，非常高兴。   True/False

4. 陈老板的公司要请人来工作。   True/False

 TASK 2. AUTHENTIC MATERIAL

In this section, you will be exposed to some authentic materials that people in China use. Look at the following border-entry form filled out by someone who went to China, and answer the questions below.

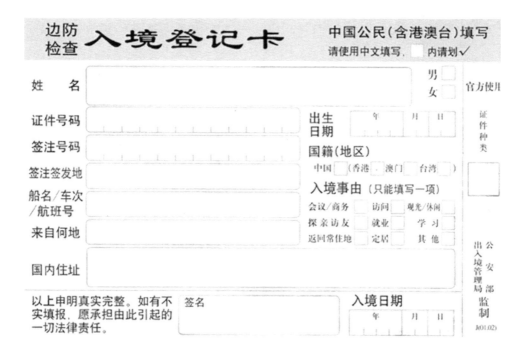

Questions

1. 你什么时候应该填这张表？

2. 你的名字写在哪儿？

3. 你的地址写在哪儿？

4. 你去中国以后，要做什么，填在哪儿？

TASK 3. SENTENCE CONSTRUCTION

Create your own questions using the phrases in the "Question" rows, and then respond using the words in the "Response" rows.

1. Ask someone how long it takes for the airplane to arrive at the Beijing airport.

   Question:　飞，才 (Verb + Time-duration)

   Response:　一个小时，就 (Verb + Time-duration)

2. Ask someone how long he/she's been working on filling out the form.

   Question:　填表 (Verb + Object + Verb + Time-duration)

   Response:　40分钟，第一次，费时间

3. Ask someone how many years he/she has been living in Beijing.

   Question:　住，年

   Response:　已经，# + 多年

4. Greet someone who just came off the airplane and ask him/her if he/she is tired.

   Question:　辛苦，累

   Response:　十几个小时，总算 (Verb 了 + # + 个小时)

 TASK 4. E-MAIL

You have just settled in at a new place after a long flight. E-mail your family to inform them of your safe arrival. In your e-mail, you should also include information about your trip. How long was the flight? Did you sleep at all during it? Did you eat? How was the food on the airplane? Did someone pick you up at the airport? Be sure to use the "Verb + Time-duration" structure.

25
体检
Getting a Physical Examination

 听力练习 (Tīnglì Liànxí)
Listening Exercises

 TASK 1. BINGO

In this section, you will hear various Chinese phrases and sentences. Demonstrate your understanding of them by numbering their English counterparts in the order in which you hear them.

A. Phrases

1 to go to the clinic for a physical
2 to lack energy
3 to prevent getting a cold
4 nationality, age, and gender
5 to measure blood pressure
6 good health
7 to not get sick
8 body height and weight
9 a headache
10 to have a fever
11 need treatment
12 not accustomed/used to
13 to get a cold
14 to prescribe medicine
15 hot weather
16 jet lag

15, 7, 1, 3, 10, 16, 8,
9, 4, 5, 14, 2, 6, 11,
12, 13

B. Sentences

1 I am in very good health; it has been two years since I was ill.
2 First let me measure your height and weight.
3 He is sick and does not feel well.
4 Please fill in your name, age, gender, and nationality.
5 I've had a physical recently.
6 Please help me pick up a form at the window on the right-hand side.
7 I have a little stomachache.
8 Over the next few days you should get a lot of rest, and don't forget to take the medicine.
9 I've got a cold, have no energy, and don't feel like eating anything.

2, 6, 9, 7, 1,
4, 8, 3, 5

🎧💻 TASK 2. SHORT CONVERSATIONS

Listen to the short conversations. Select the correct answer for each question from the choices provided.

1. 看过 / 没看过
2. 做过 / 没做过
3. 男的 / 女的
4. 要 / 不要
5. 男的 / 女的

🎧💻 TASK 3. MONOLOGUE

Listen to the two passages and answer the questions below.

Passage 1

1. What is this passage about?

    a) Chen Xiaoyun is sick.

    b) Li Lili is sick.

    c) Li Lili cares very much about Chen Xiaoyun's health condition.

    d) Chen Xiaoyun's mom cares very much about Chen Xiaoyun's health condition.

2. Where does the event mentioned in the passage occur?

    a) at Chen Xiaoyun's house

    b) at the clinic

    c) at school

    d) none of the above

Passage 2

1. What is the man talking about?

    a) The man is eager to fill out the form.

    b) The man does not want to fill out the form.

    c) The man does not know how to fill out the form.

    d) It is very easy for the man to fill out the form.

2. Who is the speaker?

   a) A teacher who is not feeling well.

   b) A student who just returned to school from a break.

   c) A freshman who just arrived at the school.

   d) An employee who works at the school clinic.

🎧💻 TASK 4. DIALOGUE

Listen to the dialogue and answer the questions below.

1. What is this dialogue about?

   a) visiting the sick

   b) the woman's health

   c) the man's health

   d) none of the above

2. How effective is the medicine provided by the doctor for high blood pressure?

   a) very effective

   b) it does not work

   c) it worked for a while

   d) none of the above

3. What did the doctor say is the reason for the man's mother's high blood pressure?

   a) She does not exercise.

   b) She does not take medication.

   c) She eats too much meat.

   d) She has reached an age where this is very common.

4. Which of the following is correct?

   a) The man's mother's blood pressure has already returned to normal.

   b) The man's mother has become a vegetarian.

   c) The man's mother believes that she should do physical exercise.

   d) All of the above.

口语练习(Kǒuyǔ Liànxí)

Speaking Exercises

 TASK 1. SUBSTITUTION

Familiarize yourself with basic sentence patterns by substituting the given phrases into the following sentences.

1. 你以前(得)过(胃病)吗？

   我没(得)过(胃病)。

用	筷子
尝	林师傅的拿手菜
沏	姜茶
办	签证

2. 你去过(学校的医务所)没有？

   我去过(两次)。

中国大使馆	几次
新开的那家饭馆	两、三次
学校旁边的那个茶馆	好几次
我家对面的那个咖啡馆	好多次

3. 你去学校的医务所(检查)过(身体)吗？

   我去年(检查)过一次。今年还没(检查)过呢。

量	血压
看	病
量	身高
称	体重

4.（学校的体检表格）你看过了吗？

我已经看过（两遍）了，还是不懂。还想再看一遍。

那本中文小说	好几遍
那张报纸	好多遍
那本杂志	一、两遍
那个成语故事	两、三遍

5. 你多久没（生病）了？

我已经（一年多）没（生病）了。

头疼	一个多月
感冒	半年多
锻炼	几个星期
看电视新闻	好几天

6. 他有点儿事，要（离开）（学校）（两，三天）。

他以前（离开）过（学校）那么长时间吗？

去	上海	二十多天
来	四川	十七、八天
离开	北京	二、三十天

🎧💻 TASK 2. QUICK RESPONSE

The following exercise will challenge your listening and speaking abilities and help you to develop good conversational skills.

A. Answering Questions

Listen to the following questions and provide an answer to each one. If you don't know a word, try to guess its meaning from the context, rather than looking it up. Remember, both speed and accuracy are important!

1. 你最近身体怎么样？

2. 你现在哪儿不舒服？

3. 你今年做过体检没有？做过几次？

4. 你去你们学校的医务所体检的时候，都要办什么手续？

B. Asking Questions

Listen to the following statements and follow the hints in the right-hand column to ask a related question for each statement. Try to avoid using the 吗-type question.

	Hints
1. 我没去过(学校的医务所)。	(Verb 过…吗？)
2. 我来中国以前检查过一次身体。	(Verb 过…没有)
3. 我最近称过一次体重。	(Verb 过…吗？)
4. 我最近感冒过两次。	(Verb 过…没有)

🎧💻 TASK 3. GUIDED ROLE-PLAYING

Listen to the following dialogues between two native speakers. Then select Role A or Role B and have a dialogue with the computer. After familiarizing yourself with the conversation, construct and record your own dialogue by replacing as many words as possible with related terms. Be creative, but be careful not to disrupt the structure of the conversation!

1. Getting a Physical

A: 你刚才是不是去医务所看病了？

B: 没有。我已经很多年没看过病了。我刚才是去医务所做体检。

A: 你没病，为什么要去医务所做体检？

B: 我觉得如果有病应该治疗，没病应该预防啊。

A: 你体检怎么样？有什么病吗？

B: 没有。一切正常。

2. Are You Feeling Better?

A: 你病好了吗？

B: 没有。还是头疼，发烧，没精神，也不想吃饭。

A: 你去学校的医务所看过病了没有？

B: 看过了。心脏，血压都很正常。

A: 最近感冒的人很多。你是不是感冒了？医生给你开药方了吗？

B: 医生说是感冒。不用吃药。要多喝水。过一个星期就好了。

TASK 4. PICTURE DESCRIPTION

Describe the pictures below using the grammar and the vocabulary you learned in this lesson. Use your imagination!

 读写练习(Dú Xiě Liànxí)
Reading/Writing Exercises

 TASK 1. SHORT STORY

Read the story and answer the True/False questions that follow.

下班以后是我自己的时间

阿乐这几个月总是觉得他心脏跳得很快。平时他很少生病，已经有两年多没有看过病了。上个星期去看过好几次病。血压量过了，心脏检查过了，心电图也做过了。一切都正常。但是他还是觉得自己得了心脏病。他很害怕，在家休息，好几天没去上班了。一天，阿笑来看阿乐。他看阿乐那副没有精神的样子，很着急。他对阿乐说："你没有大病。应该多锻炼锻炼身体。也许过几个星期，你的病自己就会好了。"阿乐说："我上班可紧张了。要工作，要吃饭，还要看病。上哪儿去找时间锻炼身体啊！"阿笑说："下班以后你为什么不去锻炼身体呢？"阿乐回答说："下班以后是我自己的时间，我要休息，还要看电视呢。"

Supplementary Vocabulary

1. 平时	píngshí	*adv.*	ordinarily, usually
2. 害怕	hàipà	*adj.*	to be afraid
3. 副	fù	*m.w.*	m.w. for a set of something, m.w. for facial expression
4. 可…了…	kě…le…		very

Questions

1. 阿乐有很长时间没看过病了。他觉得身体不舒服，在家休息，没去看病。   True/False

2. 阿乐很怕自己得了大病，但是他的身体没有大问题。   True/False

3. 阿乐很注意自己的身体健康，所以他要叫阿笑多锻炼身体。   True/False

4. 阿乐非常不喜欢锻炼身体，他觉得锻炼是一种工作。   True/False

📋 TASK 2. AUTHENTIC MATERIAL

In this section, you will be exposed to some authentic materials that people use in China. Look at the following physical check-up form used in a Chinese clinic and answer the questions below.

外 国 人 体 格 检 查 记 录

姓名	性别 □男 □女	出生日期　　年　月　日	照
现 在 通 讯 地 址		血 型	片
国　籍	出 生 地 址		

过 去 是 否 患 有 下 列 疾 病：（ 每 项 后 面 请 回 答 " 否 " 或 " 是 " ）

斑 疹 伤 寒	□No □Yes	菌 病	□No □Yes
小 儿 麻 痹 症	□No □Yes	布 氏 杆 菌 病	□No □Yes
白　喉	□No □Yes	病 毒 性 肝 炎	□No □Yes
猩 红 热	□No □Yes	产 褥 期 链 球 菌 感 染	□No □Yes
回 归 热	□No □Yes		
伤 寒 和 付 伤 寒	□No □Yes	流 行 性 脑 脊 髓 膜 炎	□No □Yes

过 去 是 否 患 有 下 列 危 及 公 共 秩 序 和 安 全 的 病 症：（ 每 项 后 面 请 回 答 " 否 " 或 " 是 " ）

毒 物 瘾		□No □Yes
精 神 错 乱		□No □Yes
精 神 病	躁 狂 型	□No □Yes
	妄 想 型	□No □Yes
	幻 觉 型	□No □Yes

| 身 高 | 厘米 体 重 | 公斤 血 压 | 毫米 |

发 育 情 况	营 养 情 况	颈 部
视 力　左　右	矫 正 视 力　左　右	眼
辨 色 力	皮肤	淋 巴 结
耳	鼻	扁 桃 体
心	肺	腹　部

Questions

1. 这张表是给什么人填的？
2. 想知道填表的人得过什么病，应该看哪几格？
3. 想知道填表的人多高、多重，应该看哪几格？
4. 想知道填表的人血压正常不正常，应该看哪几格？

💻 TASK 3. SENTENCE CONSTRUCTION

Create your own sentences using the phrases in the "Statement" rows, and then respond using the words in the "Response" rows.

1. Ask someone if he/she has had a physical check-up after he/she arrived in China.

   Statement: 以后，检查（来 Place + Time-duration, Verb 过）

   Response: 健康，体检（Time-duration + 没 Verb 了）

2. Ask someone in what way he/she is feeling unwell.

   Statement: 病了，舒服

   Response: 头疼，精神

3. Ask someone if he/she knows what preventive measures the Chinese use to prevent getting a cold.

   Statement: 中国人，预防？

   Response: 姜，姜沏的茶（多 + Verb, Verb 过, 次）

4. Ask if someone has seen the doctor for his/her high blood pressure.

   Statement: 血压，看病（Verb 过）

   Response: 两次，药方（Verb 过, 次）

 TASK 4. E-MAIL

You have been studying and working in China, and you have not had a chance to get a physical for more than a year. Your parents are very concerned about your health. Under duress, you had a physical examination last week. You are now writing an e-mail to your parents telling them physical examinations in China, based both on what you know and the experience you had. Please provide as much detail as you can. What is the procedure for doing a physical? What tests, if any, did the doctor do for you? What were the results? Did the doctor give you any advice after the physical? Be creative, and don't forget to use the grammar and vocabulary from this lesson!

26
谈季节，谈天气
Seasons and the Weather

 听力练习(Tīnglì Liànxí)
Listening Exercises

 TASK 1. BINGO

In this section, you will hear various Chinese phrases and sentences. Demonstrate your understanding of them by numbering their English counterparts in the order in which you hear them.

A. Phrases

to go to a park

to be windy and rainy

more than twenty degrees below zero

neither cold nor hot

no need to take an umbrella

very low temperature

the weather forecast

clear, fine weather turning into cloudy weather

the four seasons

cloudy turning clear

(becoming) warmer and warmer

both cool and comfortable

the best season

pretty tree leaves and green grass

thirty degrees Celsius

neither too long nor too short

B. Sentences

Fall has come, and the leaves have all turned red.

The weather forecast said it was going to rain today, but now it has cleared up.

Spring is here now, and all the grass has turned green.

There are often heavy snowfalls here in the winter.

We should find some time to go have fun in the park.

There was no wind just a moment ago, but now the wind has started.

The prediction of this specialist is not accurate.

The temperature in the summer can get to forty degrees in Beijing.

The rain has stopped. Let's go now.

🎧💻 TASK 2. SHORT CONVERSATIONS

Listen to the short conversations. Select the correct answer for each question from the choices provided.

1. 想/不想
2. 喜欢/不喜欢
3. 冬天/秋天
4. 准确/不准确
5. 住过/没住过

🎧💻 TASK 3. MONOLOGUE

Listen to the two passages and answer the questions below.

Passage 1

1. What season is this?

    a) spring

    b) summer

    c) fall

    d) winter

2. Which one of the following best describes today's weather?

    a) It is warm.

    b) It is raining.

    c) It is windy and snowing.

    d) None of the above.

Passage 2

1. How many days does this weather forecast cover?

    a) four

    b) five

    c) six

    d) seven

2. Which one of the following statements is correct?

   a) Today's weather is good.

   b) Tomorrow's temperature is higher than today's.

   c) It is going to rain on Thursday.

   d) There will be no rain this weekend.

🎧💻 TASK 4. DIALOGUE

Listen to the dialogue and answer the questions below.

1. Who calls whom?
   a) 李丽莉 calls 陈小云.
   b) 陈小云 calls 吴文德.
   c) 吴文德 calls 陈小云.

   d) None of the above.

2. During the phone conversation,
   a) 吴文德 invites 陈小云 and 李丽莉 to a park.
   b) 陈小云 invites 李丽莉 and 吴文德 to a park.
   c) 李丽莉 invites 吴文德 and 陈小云 to a park.

   d) None of the above.

3. According to 陈小云, what is the weather going to be like this weekend?

   a) It is going to rain on both Saturday and Sunday.

   b) It is going to rain on Saturday but not Sunday.

   c) It is going to rain on Sunday but not Saturday.

   d) It will be clear all weekend.

4. According to 吴文德, what is the weather forecast?

   a) It is going to rain on both Saturday and Sunday.

   b) It is going to rain on Saturday but not Sunday.

   c) It is going to rain on Sunday but not Saturday.

   d) It will be clear all weekend.

口语练习(Kǒuyǔ Liànxí)

Speaking Exercises

 TASK 1. SUBSTITUTION

Familiarize yourself with basic sentence patterns by substituting the given phrases into the following sentences.

1. 刚才(下大雨)，现在(不下)了。

    我们可以去公园了。

刮大风	小
下小雪	停
是阴天	是晴天
很冷	不那么冷

2. (春天)是不是到了？

    是啊。天气越来越(暖和)了。

夏天	热
秋天	凉快
冬天	冷

3. 你那儿今天天气怎么样？

    我这儿今天又(刮风)又(下雨)。

阴	冷
热	闷
凉快	舒服
下雪	刮风

4. 明天(最高温度)多少度？

    明天(最高温度)摄氏(三十二)度。

最低温度	二十七

最低温度能达到　零下二十多

最高气温能达到　四十多

5. 你(会跳舞)吗？

我以前不(会跳)，现在(会跳)了。

喜欢吃中国饭　　喜欢吃

爱唱歌　　　　　爱唱

想去中国　　　　想去

愿意谈对象　　　愿意谈

🎧💻 TASK 2. QUICK RESPONSE

The following exercise will challenge your listening and speaking abilities and help you to develop good conversational skills.

A. Answering Questions
Listen to the following questions and provide an answer to each one. If you don't know a word, try to guess its meaning from the context, rather than looking it up. Remember, both speed and accuracy are important!

1. 你最喜欢什么季节？为什么？

2. 你喜欢今天的天气吗？为什么？

3. 你听了今天的天气预报没有？你给我们说一说，好吗？

4. 你们那儿夏天最高气温能达到多少度？冬天最低气温能达到多少度？

B. Asking Questions
Listen to the following statements and follow the hints in the right-hand column to ask a related question for each statement. Try to avoid using the 吗-type question.

	Hints
1. 昨天气温说不定都到了摄氏40多度了。	（多少度）
2. 现在是春天了，天气越来越暖和了。	（暖和不暖和）
3. 处暑以后天气才会开始越来越凉快。	（什么时候）
4. 天气预报说星期六晴，有小风。	（怎么样）

🎧💻 TASK 3. GUIDED ROLE-PLAYING

Listen to the following dialogues between two native speakers. Then select Role A or Role B and have a dialogue with the computer. After familiarizing yourself with the conversation, construct and record your own dialogue by replacing as many words as possible with related terms. Be creative, but be careful not to disrupt the structure of the conversation!

1. Talking about the Four Seasons

   A: 春、夏、秋、冬，你最喜欢哪个季节？

   B: 我最喜欢春天。那时候，天气暖和了，花儿都 开了，草也绿了…多漂亮啊！

   A: 我觉得秋天最好。天气不冷也不热。树叶都开始红了，又舒服又漂亮。

   B: 如果冬天不冷。我也喜欢冬天。下雪的时候，白树，白房子…好看极了。

   A: 我也喜欢夏天。因为我这个人，怕冷不怕热。

2. Talking about the Weather

   A: 今天的天气真冷，现在外边的气温已经是零下二十几度了吧。

   B: 没有那么冷吧。天气预报说今天最低温度是零下20度。

   A: 今天最高温度是多少？

   B: 最高温度是零度。

   A: 明天会不会暖和一些？

   B: 不知道。明天是阴天，有雪，说不定还会刮大风。

   A: 唉，冬天太长了。春天什么时候才能来啊。

TASK 4. PICTURE DESCRIPTION

Describe the pictures below using the grammar and the vocabulary you learned in this lesson. Use your imagination!

读写练习 (Dú Xiě Liànxí)
Reading/Writing Exercises

 TASK 1. SHORT STORY

Read the story and answer the True/False questions that follow.

下次来，我们不要带这么多东西

有一次，阿笑和阿乐要去山里玩，阿乐问阿笑山里的天气好不好，阿笑说不好，有时候天晴，有时候是天阴，有时候刮风，有时候下雨，有时候还下雪。阿笑告诉阿乐多带些衣服。再带上一把伞和一顶帽子。春夏秋冬的衣服都应该带几件，因为山里边的气候变化很大，一会儿冷，一会儿热。冷的时候气温能达到零下十几度，热的时候气温能达到四十几度。阿乐准备好东西以后，就跟阿笑一起去山里玩了。

两个人在山里玩得非常高兴。阿乐回家以后就给阿笑打电话说："我们明年应该再来玩一次。不过下次来，我们不要带这么多东西，太重了。我们应该下雪的时候带冬天的衣服，下雨的时候带伞，刮风的时候戴帽子，好不好？"阿笑说："好是好，那我们一天要回多少次家去取东西呢？"

Supplementary Vocabulary

1. 山	shān	*n.*	mountain
2. 带上	dài shàng	*v.comp.*	to bring with
3. 气候	qìhòu	*n.*	climate
4. 变化	biànhuà	*n.*	change
5. 重	zhòng	*adj.*	heavy
6. 好是好…	hǎo shì hǎo	*phr.*	It is good but…

Questions

1. 阿笑和阿乐去山里玩儿的时候，带了很多衣服。　　　　True/False

2. 阿笑不喜欢去山里玩儿，因为要带的衣服太多了。　　　True/False

3. 山里一天可能会有春、夏、秋、冬四季的气候。　　　　True/False

4. 山里最高气温和最低气温差四十度。　　　　　　　　True/False

📖 TASK 2. CULTURAL KNOWLEDGE

After reading the passage, write responses to the questions below in your own words.

中国的二十四个节气

在谈中国的季节和天气的时候，不要忘了中国每个月还有两个节气。节气可以告诉大家每个月的季节和气候，每个节气都有自己的名字和自己的意思。

例如：小暑的意思是天气开始越来越热，处暑是热的天气快要过去了。大暑，大寒是一年最热和最冷的时候。小雪，大雪是说下雪的季节到了。如果我告诉你"立"是"开始"的意思，你知道立春，立夏，立秋，立冬是什么意思吗？

这些节气还挺有意思的，对吗？你有时间的时候，找一本真正的中国日历看一看。真正的中国日历上会告诉大家，每个月都有哪两个节气，每个节气是从哪一天开始。如果你很好奇，想知道每个节气都是什么意思，请查看你的光盘(读写练习1)。在光盘上，我们给大家提供了二十四个节气的定义，还有一个中国电子日历的网址。

Supplementary Vocabulary

1.	节气	jiéqì	*n.*	the twenty-four "solar periods" into which the year is divided; traditionally thought to indicate the passing of the seasons and considered important in agricultural cycles
2.	日历	rìlì	*n.*	calendar
3.	光盘	guāngpán	*n.*	CD (compact disk)
4.	定义	dìngyì	*n.*	definition
5.	网址	wǎngzhǐ	*n.*	Internet address

Questions

1. 请你说一说为什么中国日历上有"节气。"
2. 你知道"立春，""处暑，""小雪，""大寒"是什么意思吗？

🖥 TASK 3. AUTHENTIC MATERIAL

In this section, you will be exposed to some authentic materials that people use in China. Read the following weather forecast from a Chinese newspaper, and answer the questions.

星期一，五月九日

天气预报

今天白天晴转多云，北风转南风一到二级，
最高气温摄氏36度，最低气温摄氏30度。
今天夜间有雾，南风转北风二到三级，
最低气温摄氏22度。

以下是本週的天氣預報：

星期二	多云	23—35摄氏度
星期三	晴转暴雨	29—37摄氏度
星期四	阴转小雨	23—25摄氏度
星期五	阴间多云	29—33摄氏度
星期六	多云间雨	28—34摄氏度
星期日	晴	28—32摄氏度

Questions

1. 今天白天最高气温和晚上最低差了多少度？
2. 白天刮什么风？晚上刮什么风？
3. 这个星期我们哪天可以去公园玩？
4. 你觉得星期三做什么最好？

TASK 4. E-MAIL

You have been studying abroad for over a year now, and you miss your friends at home. E-mail your friends, and describe the weather in your current city during each of the four seasons. Does it usually start to snow at a certain time of year? Does it ever snow? Do you usually have lots of rain? Do you spend the whole summer trying to get out of the heat? What kind of weather is typical? Tell them which of the seasons is your favorite and why. Don't forget to use the grammar and vocabulary we learned in this lesson!

27

去邮局

Mail and the Post Office

 听力练习 (Tīnglì Liànxí)
Listening Exercises

 TASK 1. BINGO

In this section, you will hear various Chinese phrases and sentences. Demonstrate your understanding of them by numbering their English counterparts in the order in which you hear them.

A. Phrases

the clerk in the post office

to fill out a package form

to point at an envelope

to sell stamps

the names of the recipient/addressee

a few mailmen

so cheap

to send airmail

to pick up a package

to mail by air or by sea

to weigh something

to choose a postcard

the sender's address

service items

to have no identification

business hours

B. Sentences

A sign is hanging on the door of the post office.

How much does it cost to send a letter to the USA via airmail?

Would you please weigh the package?

The recipient's name and address are written on the upper part of the envelope.

My friend is carefully selecting postcards.

The post office's business hours are written on the sign.

Several types of postcards are inside the (glass) counter.

The salesperson smiled and said, "This must be your parcel."

At some windows (you can) mail a package and, at others, send a registered letter.

🎧💻 TASK 2. SHORT CONVERSATIONS

Listen to the following short conversations. Select the correct answer for each question from the choices provided.

1. 男的／女的
2. 卖／不卖
3. 填了／没有
4. 对／不对
5. 都是／不都是

🎧💻 TASK 3. MONOLOGUE

Listen to the two passages and answer the questions below.

Passage 1

1. What is this passage about?

   a) The speaker's friend has blue eyes.

   b) The speaker's friend does not know if the speaker would like Chinese stamps.

   c) The speaker's friend talks about his experience in a Chinese post office.

   d) None of the above.

2. Which of the following is correct?

   a) The speaker's friend enjoyed his experience in the post office.

   b) The speaker's friend sent the speaker some stamps.

   c) The speaker's friend only spoke Chinese in the post office that day.

   d) None of the above.

Passage 2

1. What is the main focus here?

   a) The woman cannot read the signs in a Chinese post office.

   b) The woman describes her first experience in a Chinese post office.

   c) The woman believes that her Chinese is very good.

   d) None of the above.

2. Which of the following is correct?

   a) The woman goes to the post office to mail a package.

   b) The woman fills out a form before sending registered mail.

   c) It is fairly easy for the woman to fill out the form in a post office.

   d) None of the above.

🎧💻 TASK 4. DIALOGUE

Listen to the dialogue and answer the questions below.

1. What is the main topic of this conversation?

   a) the location of the post office

   b) the post office hours

   c) the purpose of going to the post office that day

   d) none of the above

2. What is the relationship between the two speakers?

   a) husband and wife

   b) teacher and student

   c) boyfriend and girlfriend

   d) two friends

3. Which of the speakers will go to the post office?

   a) the man

   b) the woman

   c) both of them

   d) neither of them

4. Which of the following is correct?

   a) The man is going to the post office to mail a letter.

   b) The man knows how to write his address in Chinese.

   c) The woman knows how to write her address in Chinese.

   d) The woman wants to ship her packages by airmail to reduce the cost.

口语练习(Kǒuyǔ Liànxí)
Speaking Exercises

🎧📖 **TASK 1. SUBSTITUTION**

Familiarize yourself with basic sentence patterns by substituting the given phrases into the following sentences.

1. 她为什么老是(指)着(她填的那个包裹单)?

穿	她刚买的那件衣服
拿	她的学生证
想	谈对象的事
看	桌上的那个菜

2. 你弟弟现在在干什么呢?

   他在(慢慢)地(填表)呢。

认真	复习
高兴	跳舞
紧张	考试
细心	修电脑

3. 你喜欢怎么(做作业)?

   我喜欢(听着音乐)(做作业)。

看小说	喝着咖啡
学习	看着电视
做饭	唱着歌
练习口语	听着录音

4. (柜台上放)着什么?

   (柜台上放)着(一封挂号信。)

壁柜里收	几件衣服

窗口上挂　　一张照片

大门外停　　一辆车

明信片上写　他朋友的地址

5. (邮局)的(窗口)都开着没有？

有的开着，有的没开着。

教室　　　　那几个录音机

商店　　　　那些电视

宿舍　　　　门

他们　　　　手机

6. 我先(取钱)，然后再去(买邮票)。

我觉得你应该先(买邮票)然后再(取钱)。

吃饭　　　　上课

喝咖啡　　　做饭

听音乐　　　做作业

看小说　　　看电影

🎧💻 TASK 2. QUICK RESPONSE

The following exercise will challenge your listening and speaking abilities and help you to develop good conversational skills.

A. Answering Questions

Listen to the following questions and provide an answer to each one. If you don't know a word, try to guess its meaning from the context, rather than looking it up. Remember, both speed and accuracy are important!

1. 中国的邮局都有什么服务项目？

2. 中国信封的地址应该怎么写？

3. 在中国寄东西，都有一些什么手续？

4. 你寄包裹喜欢寄航空还是海运？为什么？

B. Asking Questions

Listen to the following statements and follow the hints in the right-hand column to ask a related question for each statement. Try to avoid using the 吗-type question.

		Hints
1.	我有学生证，学生证也是证件。	（有没有）
2.	海运便宜，我寄海运。	（还是）
3.	我要柜台里边左边的那种明信片。	（哪种）
4.	寄包裹、取包裹都在一号窗口。	（几号）

🎧💻 TASK 3. GUIDED ROLE-PLAYING

Listen to the following dialogues between two native speakers. Then select Role A or Role B and have a dialogue with the computer. After familiarizing yourself with the conversation, construct and record your own dialogue by replacing as many words as possible with related terms. Be creative, but be careful not to disrupt the structure of the conversation!

1. Mailing a Package

    A: 请问，寄包裹在几号窗口？

    B: 寄包裹，取包裹都在这儿。您要寄什么？

    A: 我想给我妈妈寄一个生日礼物。这是我填的包裹单。

    B: 我来称一下儿您的包裹的重量。您要寄航空还是海运？

    A: 航空快，寄航空吧。麻烦您再给我拿五张邮票。

    B: 买邮票在五号窗口。

2. Sending a Registered Letter

    A: 请问，你这儿能寄挂号信吗？

    B: 能寄。您看我窗口的牌子上写着"航空信—挂号信—邮票"。

    A: 我想寄一封航空挂号信。但是我不知道怎么寄。

    B: 这是航空信封，您还要填一张挂号单。

    A: 麻烦您告诉我一下儿地址应该怎么写。

    B: 信封的上边写收信人的地址，下边写寄信人的地址。

    A: 谢谢。

TASK 4. PICTURE DESCRIPTION

Describe the pictures below using the grammar and the vocabulary you learned in this lesson. Use your imagination!

 读写练习(Dú Xiě Liànxí)

Reading/Writing Exercises

 TASK 1. SHORT STORY

Read the story and answer the True/False questions that follow.

中国邮局

我的中国朋友阿笑上个月来美国旅游。他到美国的第二天就给我打电话，让我带他去一下儿邮局。我以为他要寄东西，就开车送他去邮局。

他刚进邮局门就好奇地问我："这是美国邮局吗？怎么这么小？"过了几分钟，他又笑着问我："我想打国际电话，我应该在哪儿排队呢？这个邮局怎么不卖报纸和杂志？"我耐心地告诉他说："美国邮局和中国邮局不一样，美国邮局没有打国际、国内电话的服务项目，也不卖报纸和杂志。"在我们回家的路上，阿笑高兴地对我说："老弟，我以后要来美国做生意，开几家跟中国一样大的邮局。邮局的服务项目也跟中国一样，可以卖报纸杂志，也可以打国际国内长途。"我听了以后不知道应该怎么回答他。只好开玩笑地对他说"老兄，好事多磨。你别着急，先在美国了解一下儿情况，然后再做决定好不好？""好吧。"阿笑说："可是，你在哪儿打国际国内长途呢？你在哪儿买报纸和杂志呢？邮局没有这种服务是不是很不方便？"我告诉他说："我在家里就可以打国际国内长途，报纸和杂志很多店都卖。"阿笑难过地问我："那我怎么做邮局的生意呢？"

Supplementary Vocabulary

1.	和 (跟) …不一样	hé (gēn)…bù yīyàng	*adj.*	to be different from…
2.	国际、国内	guójì, guónèi	*adj.*	international, domestic
3.	路上	lùshang	*phr.*	on the road
4.	长途	chángtú	*adj.*	long-distance
5.	好事多磨	hǎoshì duō mó	*phr.*	good things take a longer time
6.	情况	qíngkuàng	*n.*	situation, circumstance
7.	决定	juédìng	*v.*	to decide, to make a decision

Questions

1.	这是阿笑第一次去美国的邮局。	True/False
2.	在中国的邮局里，服务项目比较简单。	True/False
3.	阿笑来美国做生意的主意很聪明。	True/False
4.	阿笑觉得美国的邮局非常不方便。	True/False

TASK 2. AUTHENTIC MATERIAL

In this section, you will be exposed to some authentic materials that people use in China. Look at the following post office forms (for sending parcels and money) and answer the questions below.

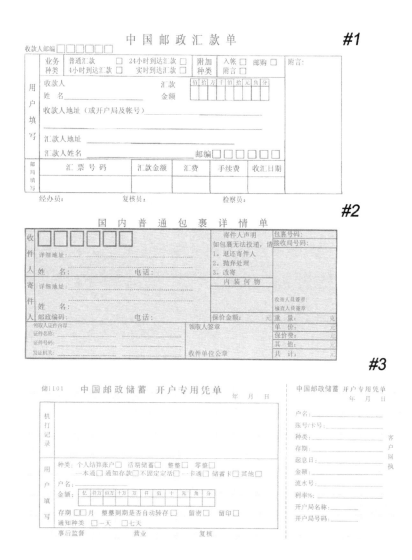

Questions

1. 哪张表格需要填你的电话号码？
2. 你要把钱寄给家里人，应该填哪张表格？
3. 你有一百块钱，想存起来，应该填哪张表格？
4. 请你把这三张表都填一填。

TASK 3. FILLING OUT FORMS

Below is the form used in Chinese post offices for mailing packages. Fill it out correctly so your package doesn't end up in the wrong place!

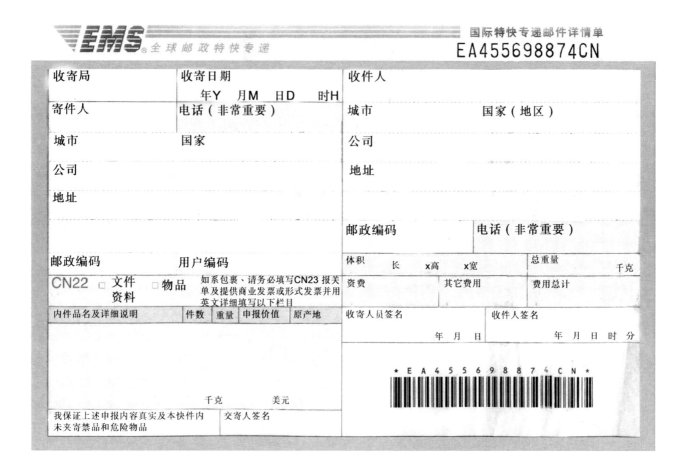

 ## TASK 4. WEB SURFING

Let's see if you know how to write Chinese addresses now. Pretend that you are sending a letter to someone in China. Surf the Web and find two authentic Chinese mailing addresses. Use one as your current address and the other as the address you are going to send your letter to. Make sure that you write the addresses correctly on an envelope.

28
找路
Knowing Where to Go

 听力练习(Tīnglì Liànxí)
Listening Exercises

 TASK 1. BINGO

In this section, you will hear various Chinese phrases and sentences. Demonstrate your understanding of them by numbering their English counterparts in the order in which you hear them.

A. Phrases

bus stop

to take the subway instead of a taxi

to be a bit more optimistic

to be unfamiliar with the route

to make a turn at the front

east, south, west, north

a tiny little mistake

change a bus after the traffic light

to take a taxi or the bus

not to go out (leave home)

to take a wrong direction

to cross an intersection

going/driving toward the hospital

to arrive at the last stop

to drive south

to get to a shopping center

B. Sentences

We probably went in the wrong direction.

We didn't hear clearly what the ticket seller was saying.

Have you bought the bus ticket yet?

This is the bus going to the Beijing Hospital; you are not on the wrong bus.

When (you) have crossed the intersection, there will be the stop for the Number 9 bus.

Walk a bit farther north; you'll be there.

I heard what the teacher said, but didn't understand (it).

If you can learn the public bus system, studying in China will be more convenient.

This is the final stop. All passengers, please take all your belongings, and be prepared to get off the bus.

🎧💻 TASK 2. SHORT CONVERSATIONS

Listen to the short conversations. Select the correct answer for each question from the choices provided.

1. 是/不是
2. 北边/南边
3. 在/不在
4. 男的/女的
5. 知道/不知道

🎧💻 TASK 3. MONOLOGUE

Listen to the two passages and answer the questions below.

Passage 1

1. What is the man talking about?

   a) the direction to his school

   b) the direction to Beijing Hospital

   c) the direction to the train station

   d) none of the above

2. How many buses does one have to take before reaching the train station?

   a) one

   b) two

   c) three

   d) four

Passage 2

1. Xiaohong and Xiaoyun arrive at the movie theater so late because:

   a) They cannot walk very fast.

   b) They take the wrong bus.

   c) They are not familiar with the subway system.

   d) All of the above.

2. Which of the following is NOT correct?

   a) Xiaoyun cannot hear the movie clearly.

   b) Xiaoyun cannot understand the movie.

   c) Xiaoyun wants to see the movie a second time.

   d) Xiaoyun does not want to see movies anymore.

🎧💻 TASK 4. DIALOGUE

Listen to the dialogue and answer the questions below.

1. What is this conversation about?

   a) whom Wu Wende saw

   b) whom Li Lili saw

   c) whom Chen Xiaoyun saw

   d) none of the above

2. Where does this conversation take place?

   a) on a bus

   b) at a hospital

   c) at the Beijing Library

   d) don't know

3. What means of transportation does Chen Xiaoyun use when she leaves the Beijing Library?

   a) bus

   b) subway

   c) subway, then bus

   d) bus, then subway

4. When does the conversation take place?

   a) before 6 A.M.

   b) at 6 A.M.

   c) shortly before 6 P.M.

   d) after 6 P.M.

口语练习 (Kǒuyǔ Liànxí)

Speaking Exercises

 TASK 1. SUBSTITUTION

Familiarize yourself with basic sentence patterns by substituting the given phrases into the following sentences.

1. 他(讲的话)你(听见)了吗？

   我没(听见)。

写的小说	看懂
教的语法	学会
借你的书	看完

2. 你(听清楚)了没有？

   这次我(听清楚)了，不会再(出错)了。

写对	写错
问清楚	坐错
准备好	考坏

3. 他的(车)还很新，怎么会(开)坏了呢？

   我也不知道他是怎么(开)坏的。

衣服	穿
帽子	戴
电脑	搞
手机	用

4. 我这个人总是(走)错(路)。

   如果你注意一点儿，就不会(走)错了。

写	地址
填	表格

坐	车
听	问题

5. 请问，到（购物中心），怎么走？

你从这儿往（前）走，到红绿灯右拐，再走十分钟就到了。

医院	东
地铁站	南
公共汽车站	西
邮局	北

6. 请问，去医院是在这儿（等车）吗？

不是，你应该在（北门）（等车）。

换车	南门
上车	东门
下车	西门
转车	下一站

🎧💻 TASK 2. QUICK RESPONSE

The following exercise will challenge your listening and speaking abilities and help you to develop good conversational skills.

A. Answering Questions

Listen to the following questions and provide an answer to each one. If you don't know a word, try to guess its meaning from the context, rather than looking it up. Remember, both speed and accuracy are important!

1. 从你住的地方走路到学校怎么走？

2. 从你住的地方坐公共汽车去购物中心怎么走？

3. 你觉得坐地铁方便吗？为什么？

4. 你喜欢坐公交，还是喜欢打的，为什么？

B. Asking Questions

Listen to the following statements and follow the hints in the right-hand column to ask a related question for each statement. Try to avoid using the 吗-type question.

	Hints
1. 你从这儿往东走，过一个十字路口就到地铁站了。	（怎么）
2. 22路公共汽车站就在前边。	（哪儿）
3. 去医院坐22路公共汽车，再换9路车。	（几路）
4. 去医院不是在这儿上车。你应该坐4路车。	（是不是）

🎧💻 TASK 3. GUIDED ROLE-PLAYING

Listen to the following dialogues between two native speakers. Then select Role A or Role B and have a dialogue with the computer. After familiarizing yourself with the conversation, construct and record your own dialogue by replacing as many words as possible with related terms. Be creative, but be careful not to disrupt the structure of the conversation!

1. Asking for Directions

A: 请问，108路公共汽车站在哪儿？

B: 从这儿往前走，到下一个十字路口，往右拐。再走一会儿就到108路车站了。……

A: 这是不是往南开的108路公共汽车站？

B: 不是，这是往北开的，开往北京医院。您去哪儿？

A: 我去邮局。我已经糊涂了。我到底应该坐往南开的，还是往北开的？

B: 去邮局应该坐往北开的。您从这儿上车，坐三站就到了。

2. Taking the Bus

A: 下一站就是终点站，请大家拿好票，准备下车。

B: 对不起，你说的话我没听清楚。是不是到终点站了？我怎么还没看见购物中心呢？我是不是坐错车了？

A: 您没坐错车，但是您坐错方向了。

B: 去购物中心不是应该往东走吗？

A: 是啊。但是我们这辆车是往西开的。

B: 那我一会儿应该在哪儿换车呢？

A: 您下车以后，过马路往左拐，过一个红绿灯，您就会看见往西开的车站。

TASK 4. PICTURE DESCRIPTION

Describe the pictures below using the grammar and the vocabulary you learned in this lesson. Use your imagination!

读写练习(Dú Xiě Liànxí)
Reading/Writing Exercises

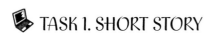

📖 TASK 1. SHORT STORY

Read the story and answer the True/False questions that follow.

我叫王大为。来中国已经一个多月了。但我还没有自己坐过公交。每次出去玩儿都是跟朋友一起打的。我觉得如果我学会了坐公共汽车，我以后去公园玩儿就能方便多了。昨天下午我决定自己坐车去颐和园看看。我的一个朋友告诉我去颐和园很容易，就在学校门口上车。坐往西开的6路公共汽车，坐四站，再换开往颐和园的332路车。终点站就是颐和园。我上了6路车，坐了四站，就换了332路，买了一张到终点站的车票。售票员话说得很快，我没听清楚，只听她最后说："一块钱。"我坐了一个小时的车，售票员报了好多站，但是都报得很快，我也没有听懂。下车的时候，那儿人很多，很热闹，我问一个人："颐和园怎么走？"他可能也没有听清楚。但是，他指着一个方向说："往前走，过了十字路，往左拐，再走十几分钟就到了。"我走了十几分钟的路，看见了一个像公园的地方。但是不像颐和园。我又找了一个人问："这是颐和园吗？"他指着那个公园大门上边的牌子说："你看。"牌子上写着：北京动物园。

Supplementary Vocabulary

1. 决定	juédìng	v.	to decide, to make a decision
2. 颐和园	Yíhéyuán	n.	The Summer Palace
3. 最后	zuìhòu	adv.	last, finally
4. 报(站)	bào (zhàn)	v.	to announce the names of the (bus) stations
5. 热闹	rènào	adj.	lively, bustling (scene)
6. 动物园	dòngwùyuán	n.	zoo

Questions

1. 颐和园在332路公共汽车终点站。   True/False

2. 从学校到颐和园，坐公共汽车要坐四站。   True/False

3. 售票员说话说得很清楚，但是王大为都听错了。   True/False

4. 王大为最后找错地方了，没有找到颐和园。   True/False

💻 TASK 2. CHENGYU STORY

Read another 成语故事 and answer the following questions.

南辕北辙

很久很久以前，有一个人要去楚国。但是楚国离他家很远，所以他买了一辆很好的马车，准备了很多很多好吃的东西，带了很多的钱就上路了。楚国在这个人家的南边，可是这个人乘着马车一直往北走。在路上，有些好心的人告诉他："你走错方向了。"他说："没关系，我的马跑得很快，我带的吃的东西也很多，我还有很多钱，我一定能到达楚国的。"他就急急忙忙地又上路了。一天早上，那个急性子的人正要上路的时候，有位好心的老人对他说："你别总是急着上路，你好好想一想，你的方向走反了。你的马跑得越快，你不就离楚国越远吗？"那人说："对不起，老大爷，我没时间跟你说话，我还要急着去楚国呢！"

Supplementary Vocabulary

1.	楚国	Chǔguó	*n.*	Chu dynasty
2.	马车	mǎchē	*n.*	horse-drawn carriage
3.	钱	qián	*n.*	money, cash
4.	上路	shàng lù	*v.obj.*	on the road
5.	急忙	jímáng	*adj.*	in a hurry, rush
6.	急性子	jíxìngzi	*adj.*	impatient
7.	越…越	yuè…yuè	*conj.*	the more…the more…

Questions

1. 请你用自己的话简单地写一遍这个故事。

2. 从这个故事里，你学会了什么？

TASK 3. AUTHENTIC MATERIAL

In this section, you will be exposed to some authentic materials that people use in China. Look at the following transportation receipts and answer the questions below.

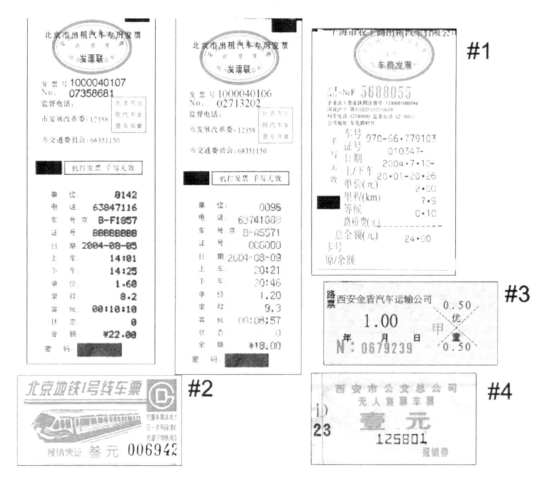

1. 这儿有几张出租车的发票？
2. 在北京坐地铁应该买哪张票？#1、#2、#3还是#4？
3. 哪一张是公共汽车票？
4. 在北京坐地铁要多少钱？

TASK 4. E-MAIL

Yesterday was the first time you ever visited your friend's house, and you had some difficulties finding his place. When you finally got there, dinner was cold. You feel bad about being late and you want to write to your friend and apologize. Consider the following when making your excuses: What form of transportation did you take? Did you get lost or take a wrong turn? Did you have to get directions from a bystander? Use the "Verb + Complement" structure when writing your message.

29

买礼物
Choosing a Gift

 听力练习(Tīnglì Liànxí)
Listening Exercises

 TASK 1. BINGO

In this section, you will hear various Chinese phrases and sentences. Demonstrate your understanding of them by numbering their English counterparts in the order in which you hear them.

A. Phrases

relatively famous

to take the elevator or to take the stairs

the customers in the shopping center

to ride a bike

to stamp a seal or to sign

one yuan and twenty-five fen

to make change

good quality

usually not expensive

to answer questions

the counter with a cash register in a department store

too cheap a gift

a scarf of 100 percent silk

to go to a department store

to use a receipt to pick up goods

to use a receipt to exchange goods

B. Sentences

This shopping center has more goods than the department store.

Of these few Chinese paintings, each one is prettier than the one before.

This scarf is of better quality than the other.

This kind of bike is less known than that one.

He does not want to answer the customers' questions.

Taking the stairs is not as fast as taking the elevator.

The pure-silk shirt is relatively light.

That cashier didn't give me my change.

The salesclerk who gave me the receipt says I cannot make an exchange.

🎧💻 TASK 2. SHORT CONVERSATIONS

Listen to the short conversations. Select the correct answer for each question from the choices provided.

1. 打的／坐地铁
2. 红的／黑的
3. 山水画／花鸟画
4. 顾客／营业员
5. 是／不是

🎧💻 TASK 3. MONOLOGUE

Listen to the two passages and answer the questions below.

Passage 1

1. What is the woman talking about?

   a) She is a very smart shopper.

   b) Her sister is a very smart shopper.

   c) Both she and her sister are very smart shoppers.

   d) Neither of them is good at finding bargains.

2. What happened yesterday?

   a) The woman bought a shirt she did not like.

   b) The woman did not like the shirt her sister bought.

   c) The woman's sister was not allowed to return the shirt she bought.

   d) The woman was not allowed to return the shirt she bought.

Passage 2

1. Which one of the following statements is correct?

   a) Until now, the speaker has never been to Beijing.

   b) The speaker has been living in Beijing for a long time.

   c) The speaker is very familiar with the streets in Beijing.

   d) The speaker is not familiar with the streets in Beijing.

2. Which one of the following statements is NOT correct?

    a) The speaker complains that the minibus was too expensive.

    b) The speaker paid four yuan for his minibus ticket.

    c) The speaker misunderstood what the ticket seller said.

    d) All of the above.

🎧💻 TASK 4. DIALOGUE

Listen to the dialogue and answer the questions below.

1. Where does the conversation take place?

    a) at a grocery store

    b) at Wu Wende's home

    c) at Chen Xiaoyun's home

    d) at Li Lili's home

2. Li Lili has invited her friends for

    a) breakfast.

    b) lunch.

    c) dinner.

    d) none of the above.

3. Which one of the following is NOT correct?

    a) Chen Xiaoyun prefers red tea to green tea.

    b) Wu Wende prefers green tea to red tea.

    c) Chen Xiaoyun likes red wine and fish.

    d) Wu Wende likes red wine and chicken.

4. Which one of the following statements is correct?

    a) Li Lili does not want to buy anything Wu Wende likes.

    b) Li Lili does not know what Wu Wende likes to eat.

    c) Li Lili does not want to go to a restaurant with Wu Wende.

    d) None of the above.

口语练习 (Kǒuyǔ Liànxí)
Speaking Exercises

 TASK 1. SUBSTITUTION

Familiarize yourself with basic sentence patterns by substituting the given phrases into the following sentences.

1. 你们谁(来)得(早)？

   他比我(来)得(早)。

走	晚
跑	快
写	慢
跳	高

2. 你(骑自行车)(骑)得比我(快)，对吗？

   哪里，我(骑)得没有你(快)。

写字	写	整齐
说中文	说	流利
唱歌	唱	好听
跳舞	跳	好看

3. 他这个人很(细心)。

   他(现在)比(以前)更(细心)了。

瘦	今年	去年
忙	这个星期	上个星期
糊涂	这个月	上个月

4. (走楼梯)有没有(坐电梯)(快)？

   没有。(坐电梯)比(走楼梯)(快)。

这套西服	那套休闲装	漂亮

这个故事	那个成语故事	好听
这个房间	那间客厅	整齐
这本小说	那个电影	好看

5. 最近(天气)是不是一(天)比一(天)(冷)了？

对，我觉得最近(天气)是一(天)比一(天)(冷)了。

他的身体	星期	健康
老师教的语法	个	难
这家百货大楼里的顾客	年	多
这儿的商店	家	贵

6. 你这儿的(自行车)多少钱一(辆)？

(八百九十块)一(辆)。

花鸟画	张	一百零八块
词典	本	五块四
衬衫	件	十块两毛五
裤子	条	二百零七块
帽子	顶	二十二块

🎧💻 TASK 2. QUICK RESPONSE

The following exercise will challenge your listening and speaking abilities and help you to develop good conversational skills.

A. Answering Questions

Listen to the following questions and provide an answer to each one. If you don't know a word, try to guess its meaning from the context, rather than looking it up. Remember, both speed and accuracy are important!

1. 你去学校上课常常骑自行车还是走路？为什么？

2. 你觉得日本车好还是美国车好？为什么？

3. 你最喜欢去哪儿买东西？小商店还是百货大楼？为什么？

4. 在中国商店买东西怎么交款？

B. Asking Questions

Listen to the following statements and follow the hints in the right-hand column to ask a related question for each statement. Try to avoid using the 吗-type question.

Hints

1. 我这儿的自行车九百零八块一辆。 （多少钱）

2. 我的英文老师教课没有我的数学老师教得那么好。 （有没有）

3. 寄纱巾比寄国画更容易。 （是不是）

4. 这个百货大楼的顾客比那个商店的顾客多。 （还是）

🎧💻 TASK 3. GUIDED ROLE-PLAYING

Listen to the following dialogues between two native speakers. Then select Role A or Role B and have a dialogue with the computer. After familiarizing yourself with the conversation, construct and record your own dialogue by replacing as many words as possible with related terms. Be creative, but be careful not to disrupt the structure of the conversation!

1. In a Department Store

   顾客：请问，你们这儿的帽子多少钱一顶？

   营业员：您喜欢哪种？这种很便宜，一顶只要六十块钱。

   顾客：您看我戴这顶帽子好看吗？

   营业员：很漂亮。这儿还有一种，比那种贵，八十块一顶。质量比刚才的那种好。但是，颜色没有刚才的那种好。

   顾客：质量第一。颜色也不比刚才的那种差。请您给我开一张发票。

   营业员：这是您的发票，请到收款台交钱。

2. At the Check-out Counter

   顾客：这是我的发票。

   营业员：八十块。

   顾客：我没有零钱，这是一百块钱。

   营业员：找您二十块钱。这是您的发票，请到柜台去取货。

   顾客：这两张发票哪张交给营业员取货？哪张是我的？

   营业员：上边的那张交给营业员，下边的是你的收据，帽子如果有问题，你可以凭收据来退换。

TASK 4. PICTURE DESCRIPTION

Describe the pictures below using the grammar and the vocabulary you learned in this lesson. Use your imagination!

 读写练习(Dú Xiě Liànxí)
Reading/Writing Exercises

 TASK 1. SHORT STORY

Read the story and answer the True/False questions that follow.

我现在去商店没有以前去得多了，但是买东西比以前买得更多。你知道为什么吗？我现在在网上买东西。我觉得在网上买东西比去商店方便。你能在很短的时间里去很多商店，有的在北京，有的在广东，有的在上海。

你想买一种商品，你能在很多地方好好地比较比较，看在哪个地方买最便宜，质量最好，牌子最有名。然后，你只要轻轻地按一下儿鼠标，那个东西就是你的了。你说这是不是比你自己去商店更方便？不过，在网上买东西也有缺点。那就是花钱花得太快。东西越便宜，你买得越多。花钱也就越厉害。你看，这个月才过了一半，我的钱已经快花完了。对了。在网上买东西还有一个大缺点，就是退换商品没有在商店容易。你得去邮局寄包裹，要花时间，还要花钱。有一次，我买了一条真丝纱巾，有一点儿小毛病，要退换。我去邮局寄了。但是，三个星期以后，他们还没有收到。最后，我又买了一条。

Supplementary Vocabulary

1.	在网上	zài wǎngshàng	*phr.*	on the Internet
2.	商品	shāngpǐng	*n.*	merchandise, goods
3.	按	àn	*v.*	to click, to press
4.	鼠标	shǔbiāo	*n.*	computer mouse
5.	缺点	quēdiǎn	*n.*	shortcoming
6.	花钱	huāqián	*v.obj.*	to spend money
7.	越…越…	yuè…yuè…	*conj.*	the more…the more…
8.	毛病	máobìng	*n.*	defect

Questions

1. 在网上买东西没有去商店买东西那么麻烦。   True/False
2. 在网上买的东西不比在商店买的便宜。   True/False
3. 在网上买东西有的时候质量没有商店买的那么好。   True/False
4. 在网上买东西不能退换。   True/False

💻 TASK 2. CHENGYU STORY

Read another 成语故事 and answer the following questions.

千里送鸿毛，礼轻情义重

很久很久以前，有一天著名的书法家王羲之从外地回家，在路上，他觉得又渴又饿，就在一家茶馆里喝了一杯茶。吃了一点东西。可是在要离开茶馆的时候，才发现自己没有带钱。王羲之很不好意思地问茶馆老板他能不能画一张画，用他的画来交茶钱。

老板不认识王羲之，但是还是同意了。王羲之看见茶馆老板的天鹅很漂亮，就画了一只天鹅。茶馆老板觉得王羲之画的天鹅跟真的一样漂亮，就把画儿挂在墙上了。过了不久，越来越多的人都跑到茶馆来看王羲之的画。茶馆的生意也越来越好。一天，有一个非常有钱的人花了很多钱从茶馆老板那儿买走了王羲之的画。茶馆老板有钱了，也不需要再开茶馆了。他心里很感谢王羲之。一天他带着自己的天鹅去找王羲之。路上刮风下雨他走得很辛苦。快到王羲之家的时候，茶馆老板觉得他的天鹅太脏了，就到一条小河边，想去洗一洗那只天鹅。可是没有想到天鹅飞走了。他的手里只有一根天鹅毛。茶馆老板只好拿着鹅毛去见王羲之。他给王羲之讲了自己为什么来，还讲了天鹅是怎么没有了的故事。王羲之听了以后，笑着对他说："千里送鹅毛，礼轻情义重。"

Supplementary Vocabulary

1. 著名	zhùmíng	*adj.*	famous
2. 书法家	shūfǎ jiā	*n.*	calligrapher
3. 王羲之	Wáng Xīzhī	*prop.n.*	a famous calligrapher in ancient China
4. 外地	wàidì	*n.*	part of the country other than where one is
5. 发现	fāxiàn	*v.*	to find out, to discover
6. 同意	tóngyì	*v.*	to agree
7. 天鹅	tiān'é	*n.*	swan
8. 脏	zāng	*adj.*	dirty
9. 河	hé	*n.*	river
10. 没想到	méi xiǎngdào	*phr.*	have not expected...
11. 根	gēn	*m.w.*	for long and thin things
12. 毛	máo	*n.*	fur, hair
13. 只好	zhǐ hǎo	*phr.*	have to, have nothing to do but...

Questions

1. 请你写一下儿书法家王羲之和茶馆老板的关系是什么？

2. 请你用自己的话写一下儿"千里送鹅毛，礼轻情义重"是什么意思？

🎧💻 TASK 3. AUTHENTIC MATERIAL

In this section, you will be exposed to some authentic materials that people use in China. Look at the following receipts from different stores and answer the questions below.

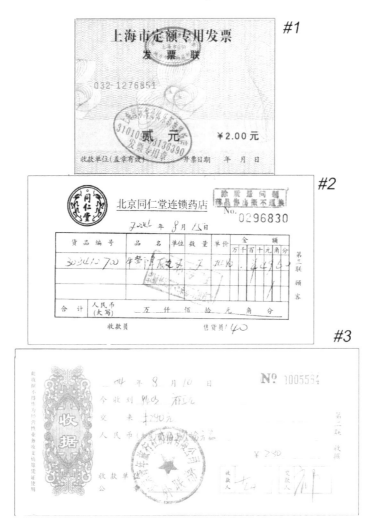

Questions

1. 你能说一说哪一个顾客买的东西最便宜，#1、#2还是#3？
2. 哪一个顾客买的东西最贵，#1、#2还是#3？
3. 哪一张收据上面有顾客的名字？
4. 这三张发票上都盖了章了吗？

💻 TASK 4. E-MAIL

You are e-mailing a friend about your different shopping experiences. Discuss the advantages and disadvantages of shopping in stores and shopping online. Be sure to include the comparative structures 比/不比 and 有/没有, and the adverbs 比较，更，and 最，as you compare the two.

30
逛夜市
Browsing at the Night Market

 听力练习(Tīnglì Liànxí)
Listening Exercises

 TASK 1. BINGO

In this section, you will hear various Chinese phrases and sentences. Demonstrate your understanding of them by numbering their English counterparts in the order in which you hear them.

A. Phrases

to browse at the night market   good at bargaining

ability to negotiate price   to do business at a loss

huge discount   fifty percent off

on both sides of streets   to set up a booth

jacket and sweater   to not make extra money

to grow slender   to guarantee the quality

perfect fit   not too loose, not too tight

movie star   to watch the crowds

B. Sentences

This gray jacket is three centimeters longer than the blue jacket.

This one is the same length as the other one, but the width is not the same.

These blue jeans are ten yuan cheaper than the black jeans.

This street vendor sells things a lot faster than the other one.

This sweater fits me better than the other one.

He made one hundred yuan more today than yesterday.

The night market we browsed today was more bustling than the one we visited yesterday.

This booth sells sweaters of a different length than that booth.

This street vendor is not as much of a smooth talker as the other.

🎧💻 TASK 2. SHORT CONVERSATIONS

Listen to the short conversations. Select the correct answer for each question from the choices provided.

1. 九点/七点
2. 合适/不合适
3. 是/不是
4. 男的/女的
5. 男的/女的

🎧💻 TASK 3. MONOLOGUE

Listen to the passage and answer the questions below.

Passage 1

1. What is the monologue about?

   a) The man is very proud of his bargaining skills.

   b) The man is unable to lower the price.

   c) When negotiating price, the customers always win.

   d) None of the above.

2. Which one of the following statements is correct?

   a) The vendor's jeans are a lot cheaper than other jeans at the night market.

   b) The vendor is willing to sell the jeans at a lower price than his competitors.

   c) The vendor refuses to sell the jeans any cheaper.

   d) None of the above.

Passage 2

1. What is the woman talking about?

   a) She is a better bargainer than Chen Xiaoyun.

   b) Chen Xiaoyun is a better bargainer.

   c) Both of them are very good at bargaining.

   d) Neither of them is good at bargaining for a better price.

2. Which one of the following statements is correct?

   a) Chen Xiaoyun bought the sweater at thirty percent off.

   b) Chen Xiaoyun bought the sweater at seventy percent off.

   c) Chen Xiaoyun did not buy the sweater because she could not get any discount.

   d) None of the above.

🎧💻 TASK 4. DIALOGUE

Listen to the dialogue and answer the questions below.

1. Where does this dialogue take place?

   a) at Li Lili's dorm

   b) at Wu Wende's dorm

   c) at a night market

   d) at a department store

2. How many shirts has Wu Wende tried on?

   a) one

   b) two

   c) three

   d) four

3. Which one does Wu Wende like?

   a) white

   b) blue

   c) gray

   d) none of the above

4. Which one of the following is NOT correct?

   a) Wu Wende has bought a cotton shirt.

   b) Li Lili is more careful than Wu Wende.

   c) The gray shirt fits Wu Wende perfectly.

   d) All of the above.

口语练习(Kǒuyǔ Liànxí)
Speaking Exercises

 TASK 1. SUBSTITUTION

Familiarize yourself with basic sentence patterns by substituting the given phrases into the following sentences.

1. 她跟她的室友一样(苗条)吗？

   不一样。她比她的室友(胖一点)。

聪明	笨一点
重	轻一些
大	小两岁
紧张	放松多了

2. 你跟他(穿)得一样多吗？

   我比他少(穿一件毛衣)。

吃	吃一块蛋糕
赚	赚几百块钱
喝	喝一杯咖啡
背	背几个单词

3. 你(讲价钱讲)得跟他一样(棒)吗？

   他比我(讲)得(棒)得多。

说中文	说	流利
骑自行车	骑	快
写字	写	漂亮
做饭	做	好吃

4. 他的(毛衣)有没有他的(夹克)那么(贵)？

   差不多，他的(毛衣)也比较(贵)。

客厅	餐厅	大

笔记	书	多
床	椅子	舒服
中文	日语	好

5. 这（件）（毛衣）跟那（件）有什么不一样？

这（件）比那（件）（小两厘米）。

顶	帽子	大两号
条	牛仔裤	长一厘米
套	西服	短三厘米
身	休闲装	小一号

🎧💻 TASK 2. QUICK RESPONSE

The following exercise will challenge your listening and speaking abilities and help you to develop good conversational skills.

A. Answering Questions

Listen to the following questions and provide an answer to each one. If you don't know a word, try to guess its meaning from the context, rather than looking it up. Remember, both speed and accuracy are important!

1. 在商店买东西跟在夜市买东西有什么一样和不一样的地方？

2. 你喜欢在哪儿买东西？为什么？

3. 你给我们说几句讨价还价的句子，好吗？

4. 夜市的小贩和商店里的营业员有什么一样和不一样的地方？为什么？

B. Asking Questions

Listen to the following statements and follow the hints in the right-hand column to ask a related question for each statement. Try to avoid using the 吗-type question.

Hints

1. 那条蓝色的牛仔裤跟这条黑色的一样。　　　　　（有什么不一样）

2. 这件夹克跟那件夹克肥瘦一样。　　　　　　　　（一样不一样）

3. 不能再便宜了，我已经赔本了。　　　　　　　　（便宜一点儿）

4. 好吧。再少给十块钱吧，我真是没赚上几个钱。（便宜十块钱）

🎧💻 TASK 3. GUIDED ROLE-PLAYING

Listen to the following dialogues between two native speakers. Then select Role A or Role B and have a dialogue with the computer. After familiarizing yourself with the conversation, construct and record your own dialogue by replacing as many words as possible with related terms. Be creative, but be careful not to disrupt the structure of the conversation!

1. Bargaining for a Lower Price

   A: 对不起，您少找了我二十块钱。

   B: 不会吧。您刚才给我四百。我找您二十，没错儿啊？

   A: 我买了两条牛仔裤，一百七十块一条。

   B: 这种牛仔裤是一百八十块一条。

   A: 您这儿的牛仔裤怎么比那个摊子上的贵十块呢？

   B: 啊呀，我的牛仔裤和那儿的不一样，质量好多了。您看看，做得多好！

   A: 但是你这儿的牛仔裤比那儿的贵得多。我不买了。

   B: 您别走啊。我给您每条便宜五块钱，怎么样？我今天真的赔本了。

2. Buying at a Night Market

   A: 那件红色的衬衫和黑色的价钱一样吗？

   B: 不一样。红的比黑的贵三块，红的是二十六块一件。

   A: 黑的为什么比红的便宜呢？它跟红衬衫的质量不一样吗？

   B: 黑衬衫是全棉的，红衬衫是百分之百真丝的。

   A: 两件大小一样不一样？

   B: 黑的比红的大两号。

   A: 黑的比红的好看得多。但是红的比黑的质量好。我两件都买了。

   B: 一共四十九块钱。

TASK 4. PICTURE DESCRIPTION

Describe the pictures below using the grammar and the vocabulary you learned in this lesson. Use your imagination!

 读写练习 (Dú Xiě Liànxí)
Reading/Writing Exercises

 TASK 1. SHORT STORY

Read the story and answer the True/False questions that follow.

我在街上买东西的时候，非常喜欢讨价还价，所以，我觉得我讲价钱的本领还可以。但是，夜市上的小贩讲价钱的本领比我的大多了。有一天，我在一个小摊子上看见一件衬衫，挺好看的，就试了试。我穿了以后，才知道那件衬衫又肥又大，比我的毛衣还肥得多。但是那个小贩看了看，说："这件衬衫稍长一点，比你身上穿的衣服长半厘米吧。但是这件衬衫是全棉的。你回家以后，洗一洗再穿，就不会长了。"你说那个贩子油不油。

上个星期我妈妈从美国来看我。我带她去逛夜市。去以前我告诉她夜市的小贩都很油，很会赚钱，让她注意一点。要不，一定会上当受骗。我们刚到夜市，第一个小摊子的小贩就不停地对我妈妈说："我的牛仔裤最便宜，一条牛仔裤才一百五十块钱。"我妈妈听了，非常高兴。她说："啊呀，这儿的东西比美国的便宜多了。"小贩赶快说："这种牛仔裤跟你们美国的质量一样好，但是您在我这儿买，要比您在美国买少花十几个美金呢，您多买几条吧。这条黑色的一百六十块一条，那条灰的一百八十块一条。"

我妈妈好奇地问："不是每条一百五十块钱吗？"小贩说："蓝色的牛仔裤是一百五十块钱一条。"我妈妈问："黑色和灰色的牛仔裤为什么比蓝色的贵？蓝色的质量跟黑色和灰色的不一样吗？"小贩回答说："蓝色的质量跟黑色、灰色的差不多，但是因为黑色和灰色的牛仔裤比较少，所以要贵一些。"我妈妈检查了质量，又问："这条蓝牛仔裤怎么左腿比右腿要长一公分，右腿还比左腿肥一点儿。"小贩说："真的吗？那这条蓝牛仔裤应该是一百七十块钱，不应该是一百五十块钱。"我妈妈更糊涂了。她问"为什么呢？"小贩说："这条蓝牛仔裤是用手工做的。用手工做的要比用机器做的贵二十块钱，因为用手工做裤子比用机器做费时间。"

Supplementary Vocabulary

1. 腿	tuǐ	*n.*	leg
2. 手工	shǒugōng	*n.*	handwork
		adv.	by hand
3. 机器	jīqì	*n.*	machine

Questions

1. 我试穿的全棉衬衫很合适，很配我的毛衣。　　　　True/False
2. 三种颜色的牛仔裤，灰色的最贵，蓝色的最便宜。　　True/False

3. 黑色和灰色的牛仔裤比蓝色的贵是因为质量比较好。   True/False

4. 小贩说：手工做的衣服没有机器做的质量好。   True/False

 TASK 2. CHENGYU STORY

Read another 成语故事 and answer the following questions.

金玉其外，败絮其中

从前，有一个小贩子。他很会储藏水果，他能把水果保留一年，也不让水果变坏。有一天一个顾客看见他的水果很漂亮，就买了。但是，回家用刀子打开一看，水果里面全都干了，像破棉絮一样。这个顾客很生气，就来找这个小贩说："你怎么能卖这样的水果？"小贩听了，回答说：我做生意已经做了好多年了。我卖，顾客买。除了你以外，还没有别人不满意。而且，做这样的事儿的不是我一个人。再说，你有没有想过那些当官的有钱人。他们都骑着又高又大的马，每天吃很贵的大鱼大肉。他们外边看起来都很威严。但是，里面不也跟破棉絮一样吗？你为什么不去好好地研究研究他们的问题，一定要来给我找麻烦呢？

Supplementary Vocabulary

1. 金玉其外，败絮其中	jīnyù qíwài, bàixù qízhōng	*phr.*	(lit.) gold and jade on the outside, but spoiled cotton filling (of a cushion, etc.)
金		*n.*	gold
玉		*n.*	jade
其		*pron.*	his/her/its/their + n.
败		*adj.*	spoil, fail, ruin
絮		*n.*	cotton wadding
2. 储藏	chǔcáng	*v.*	to save, to preserve, to store
3. 保留	bǎoliú	*v.*	to reserve, to retain, to keep
4. 变	biàn	*v.*	to change, to turn into
5. 刀子	dāozi	*n.*	pocketknife
6. 干	gān	*adj.*	dry
7. 破	pò	*adj.*	broken, damaged

8. 棉絮	miánxù	*n.*	cotton-padded mattress
9. 生气	shēngqì	*adj.*	angry
10. 除了…以外	chúle...yǐwài	*conj.*	besides, except
11. 满意	mǎnyì	*adj.*	satisfied, pleased
12. 而且	érqiě	*conj.*	moreover, in addition
13. 当官	dāng guān	*v.obj.*	serve as an official
14. 威严	wēiyán	*adj.*	powerful and strict

Questions

1. 请用自己的话说一说金玉其外，败絮其中是什么意思？
2. 小贩子说的话对不对？为什么？
3. 顾客说的话对不对？为什么？
4. 你从这个故事里学会了什么？

TASK 3. AUTHENTIC MATERIAL

In this section, you will be exposed to some authentic materials that people use in China. Look at the following two advertisements and answer the questions below.

Questions

1. 哪家商店的东西正在降价？

2. 哪家商店卖旧货？

3. 你想在哪家商店买东西可以讨价还价？

4. 哪家商店女顾客比男顾客多？

TASK 4. E-MAIL

Choose one of the e-mail topics below.

A. You are e-mailing your friends about your Chinese studies. Use the comparative structure to discuss the following:

   1. Your comparative language skills (listening, speaking, reading, and writing)

   2. Your understanding of Chinese culture in comparison with your classmates

   3. Your teachers

   4. Time spent learning Chinese

   (Use the comparative structures "比…更/还…," "比…得多/多了/一点," "有/没有…那么/这么…," "跟…一样/不一样," and "比…早/晚/大/小 + Amount.")

B. You just came back from a Chinese night market and now you are e-mailing your friend in the U.S. comparing the Chinese night market with the U.S. flea market or farmer's market. What kinds of things are sold at each? What are the prices? What forms of money are accepted? Be sure to include what distinguishes the various markets from each other (besides the obvious: their location). What is similar about them? Don't forget to include the comparative structures you've just learned in your explanation.

31
去银行
Opening a Bank Account

 听力练习(Tīnglì Liànxí)
Listening Exercises

 TASK 1. BINGO

In this section, you will hear various Chinese phrases and sentences. Demonstrate your understanding of them by numbering their English counterparts in the order in which you hear them.

A. Phrases

to be the next client's turn

foreign currency exchange service

anytime

to use cash or traveler's checks

record of his bankbook

don't overspend

guarantor

to open an account

a deposit slip

to deposit or withdraw money

debit cards and credit cards

to not accept a credit or debit card

no ATM machine

CD or savings deposit

the bank's interest rate

exchange rate between American dollars and Chinese currency

B. Sentences

I want to open a savings account, and a Certificate Deposit as well.

When it is your turn, the number-calling machine will display your number on the screen.

Because there is someone to stand guarantor for you, you can apply for a credit card.

Only after you've opened a bank account can you apply for a debit card.

Although many big stores are taking credit cards, you should still bring some cash with you.

What is the exchange rate between Chinese currency and the U.S. dollar?

The interest rates at these banks are all the same.

I still haven't received the check my mom sent me.

Every time you deposit or withdraw money, it will be recorded in your bankbook.

🎧💻 TASK 2. SHORT CONVERSATIONS

Listen to the short conversations. Select the correct answer for each question from the choices provided.

1. 知道/不知道
2. 是/不是
3. 知道/不知道
4. 买到了/没买到
5. 有/没有

🎧💻 TASK 3. MONOLOGUE

Listen to the two passages and answer the questions below.

Passage 1

1. What is the speaker talking about?

   a) The speaker is bragging about how much money she has.

   b) The speaker has enough money to last until her mother's check arrives.

   c) The speaker has used up the money in her account.

   d) None of the above.

2. Which of the following is correct?

   a) The speaker spent all her money on a cellular phone.

   b) The speaker did not have enough money to eat at a restaurant.

   c) The speaker just received a check from her mother.

   d) None of the above.

Passage 2

1. What is the speaker talking about?

   a) The man is debating whether he should have deposited his 300 yuan.

   b) The man is debating whether he should deposit more cash.

   c) The man is wondering whether he should get another debit card.

   d) None of the above.

2. Which of the following is correct?

   a) There is 300 yuan at the speaker's home.

   b) The man's friend doesn't think he should use credit cards and debit cards.

   c) The man wants to borrow money from his friend.

   d) None of the above.

🎧💻 TASK 4. DIALOGUE

Listen to the dialogue and answer the questions below.

1. What are the two speakers talking about?

    a) whether or not the woman should purchase anything in China

    b) methods of payment if the woman purchases anything in China

    c) how to open a bank account

    d) none of the above

2. Where does the conversation take place?

    a) at a bank

    b) at a store

    c) on an airplane

    d) none of the above

3. Which of the following statements is correct?

    a) The woman has no knowledge of the Chinese banking system.

    b) The woman has ample knowledge of the Chinese banking system.

    c) The woman has limited knowledge of the Chinese banking system.

    d) None of the above.

4. Which of the following statements is NOT correct?

    a) The woman has a bank account in China.

    b) The woman does not have any cash with her.

    c) The woman wants to use her checks.

    d) The woman does not have a debit card.

口语练习(Kǒuyǔ Liànxí)
Speaking Exercises

 TASK 1. SUBSTITUTION

Familiarize yourself with basic sentence patterns by substituting the given phrases into the following sentences.

1. 你的(钱)(存)在哪儿了？

信用卡	收
车	停
画报	放
地址	写
照片	挂

2. 我昨天晚上(填表填)到十二点，才(填完)。

写作业写	写完
看书看	看完
考试考	考完
学中文学	学完
读报读	读完

3. (今天学的生词)，你(记)住了没有？

没(记)住。

今天来的客人	留
车开到红灯前边	停
那边的那个大门	关

4. 我因为(常常丢现金)，所以(总是用借记卡)。

没有钱存	没有银行帐户
常常锻炼	身体很健康

裤子太旧了   又买了一条

对地铁路线不熟悉   得打的去

5. 我虽然已经(在银行开了帐户)了，但是还没有(找到开信用卡的担保人)。

起床   洗澡

下课   做完作业

申请学校   收到录取通知书

给他留了话   接到他给我回的电话

6. 虽然(我有借记卡)，但是(我的帐号里没有钱)。

我家离大使馆很近   我还没时间办护照

老师常常给我们考试   考试都不难。

我在银行存了我的支票   银行还是不让我取钱

现在是秋天了   天气还是很热

7. 我的(银行)不但(利息高)，而且(也不收费)。

衣服   漂亮   便宜

中文字   写得好看   写得很快

室友   喜欢唱歌   喜欢跳舞

朋友   有借记卡   有信用卡

8. 不但(存钱要填表)，而且(取钱也要填表)。

我常常喝咖啡   我的室友也常常喝咖啡

我考试没考好   我的朋友也没考好

我喜欢看中文报   我哥哥也喜欢看

我去参加了舞会   我妹妹也参加了

🎧💻 TASK 2. QUICK RESPONSE

The following exercise will challenge your listening and pronunciation abilities and help you to develop good conversational skills.

A. *Answering Questions*

Listen to the following questions and provide an answer to each one. If you don't know a word, try to guess its meaning from the context, rather than looking it up. Remember, both speed and accuracy are important!

1. 哪种卡能超支？借记卡还是信用卡？

2. 什么是外卡取现？

3. 如果你有一张五百美金的支票，你想开什么帐户？为什么？

4. 在中国办信用卡你必须先做什么？

B. *Asking Questions*

Listen to the following statements and follow the hints in the right-hand column to ask a related question for each statement. Try to avoid using the 吗-type question.

	Hints
1. 借记卡和信用卡，两种卡都很方便。	（还是）
2. 轮到你的时候，叫号机会在屏幕上显示你的号码。	（什么时候）
3. 今天美金和人民币兑换率是 1 比 8.2。	（多少）
4. 存美金，你得去外汇窗口。	（哪儿）

🎧💻 TASK 3. GUIDED ROLE-PLAYING

Listen to the following dialogues between two native speakers. Select Role A or Role B and have a dialogue with the computer. After familiarizing yourself with the conversation, construct and record your own dialogue by replacing as many words as possible with related terms. Be creative, but be careful not to disrupt the structure of the conversation!

A. Opening a Bank Account

A: 麻烦你给我开一个帐户，我想存两百美金。

B: 你要存定期、还是活期？

A: 我存一年的定期，这是我的支票。

B: 你带证件了吗？

A: 带了。我这儿有护照和学生证。

B: 请稍等⋯。这是你的定期存款单。

B. Debit Card or Credit Card?

A: 麻烦你给我办一个信用卡。

B: 你在我们银行有帐户吗？

A: 有。这是我的帐户和我的证件。

B: 你填了申请表了吗？有没有担保人？

A: 对不起。我刚来这个地方，没有担保人。

B: 你得找到一个担保人，才能办信用卡。你还是先办一个借记卡吧。

TASK 4. PICTURE DESCRIPTION

Describe the pictures using the grammar and the vocabulary you learned in this lesson. Use your imagination!

读写练习(Dú Xiě Liànxí)
Reading/Writing Exercises

 TASK 1. SHORT STORY

Read the story and answer the questions that follow.

送钱包

我去年冬天去中国的时候，住在我朋友钟明那儿。一天下午，我在商店里买东西，收款台的营业员说我的借记卡的帐户里的钱不够了。我钱包里虽然有一张旅行支票，但是营业员说商店不接受支票。我因为钱包里没有现金，所以必须马上去银行兑换支票，取钱。我急急忙忙跑到银行，手续很顺利。我不但存了支票，（我的借记卡也就能用了）而且取了一些人民币。我高高兴兴地回到了商店。可是，在收款台交钱的时候，才发现我的钱包没有了。我赶快又回到银行去找钱包，又在从银行去商店的路上找，还是没有找到。钱包里不但有我的借记卡，而且还有一些现金。对了，我的钱包还有两张美国的信用卡和我在美国的学生证。我得马上取消我的那两张美国信用卡。因为现在北京有不少大商店都接受美国的信用卡。我很着急，赶快往钟明家跑，想给美国的银行打电话。我快到钟明家的时候，看见一个二十多岁的姑娘站在门外。她说她拣到了一个钱包，打开以后，看见里面有一张纸，上边写着钟明家的地址。她怕丢钱包的人着急，就到钟明家门口来等丢钱包的人。她给了我钱包以后就走了。等到她走远了，我才想到我忘记问她的名字了。

Supplementary Vocabulary

1. 钱包   qiánbāo   *n.*   wallet
2. 接受   jiēshòu   *v.*   to accept
3. 发现   fāxiàn   *v.*   to discover
4. 取消   qǔxiào   *v.*   to cancel
5. 往   wǎng   *prep.*   to, towards
6. 拣   jiǎn   *v.*   to pick up

Questions

1. 我买东西的商店不但不接受支票，而且也不收借记卡和信用卡。
   True/False

2. 如果有人拿到我的信用卡，他就可以用我的卡买东西。
   True/False

3. 因为我把我的钱包忘在钟明家里了，所以我赶快往钟明家跑。
   True/False

4. 虽然给我送钱包来的姑娘不认识钟明，但是她还是找到了钟明的家。
   True/False

 TASK 2. CHENGYU STORY

In this section, you will be exposed to a Chinese 成语故事 (chéngyǔ gùshi). A 成语 is usually a four-character phrase in Chinese. It is a humorous way of teaching people a set of morals or a piece of wisdom. A 成语故事 is a story that describes where the 成语 comes from. Read the story below and answer the following questions.

一毛不拔

中国古代的时候，有两个著名的思想家。一个叫墨翟，一个叫杨朱。墨翟觉得人和人在一起应该有一种"爱"。应该互相帮助，不应该互相残杀。有了"爱"人们就能快乐地过日子。杨朱觉得人和人之间没有真正的"爱"。每个人都应该为自己。干任何事情都要先想自己。他觉得要是我给你帮助，你也应该给我帮助。我为什么要多给别人帮助呢？

有一天墨翟的一个学生问杨朱说："如果从你身上拔一根毛，对所有的人都有帮助，你肯让别人拔吗？"杨朱回答说："拔我的一根毛是不可能对所有的人都有帮助的。"那个学生又问："如果可能的话，你愿意吗？"杨朱说："这是不可能的事。" 那个学生又问了好几次，杨朱就是不肯说他愿意。后来，人们就用"一毛不拔"来描述那些非常非常小气的人。

Supplementary Vocabulary

1. 一毛不拔	yīmáobùbá	*phr.*	(lit.) unwilling to give up even a hair; to not lift a finger to help, stingy
毛		*n.*	hair
拔		*v.*	to pull out or up
2. 著名	zhùmíng	*adj.*	famous
3. 思想家	sīxiǎng jiā	*n.*	thinker, philosopher
4. 互相	hùxiāng	*adv.*	mutually, reciprocally, each other
5. 残杀	cánshā	*v.*	to kill
6. 描述	miáoshù	*v.*	to describe
7. 小气	xiǎoqi	*adj.*	stingy

Proper Nouns

1. 墨翟	Mò Dí	a person's name
2. 杨朱	Yáng Zhū	a person's name

Questions

1. 请用你自己的话讲一讲"一毛不拔"是什么意思？
2. 请你比较一下两位思想家墨翟和杨朱。
3. 你认识一个"一毛不拔"的人吗？请你描述一下这个人。

🖳 TASK 3. AUTHENTIC MATERIAL

Below is an authentic form used in China. Complete the form, and then challenge yourself and see if you are able to answer the questions that follow.

中国银行人民币长城信用卡

申 请 表

(个人卡)

主卡申领人资料

姓名(中文及汉语拼音):		
身份证号码:		性别:
出生日期：　　年　月　日	民族:	婚否:
工作单位:		职务：部门:
单位性质：行政□　事业□　企业□　　股份公司□　　私营□		职称:
单位地址:		电话：手机：　　邮编:
家庭住址:		电话：传呼：　　邮编:
月工资：　　　　其他收入:		家庭人口:
配偶姓名:		出生日期:
单位名称:		单位电话:
对帐单寄至：　工作单位□　家庭住址□　　自取□		
其他住址:		
曾经申领过长城卡或其他信用卡：		
卡号1:		效期:
卡号2:		效期:

(注：请用黑色钢笔，正楷字体清楚填写本表，并附各申请人及联系人身份证的影印件。)

附属卡申领人资料

姓名(中文及汉语拼音):	性别:
身份证号码:	出生日期：　年　月　日
单位名称:	单位电话:
单位地址:	住宅电话:
住宅地址:	本人签字:

发卡银行资料

初审意见:		
签章:		年　月　日
发卡类型：　金卡□　普通卡□	信用额度	
卡号：主卡	有效期	
附属卡1	有效期	
附属卡2	有效期	
保证金帐号:	金额	
申请号：□ □ □ □ □ □		
备注:		
复审意见:		
签章:		年　月　日
持卡人签领:		
		年　月　日
其他记录:		

Questions

1. 填表的人要申请什么？
2. 申请人需要填哪些地址？
3. 申请过这种卡的人还能不能再申请？
4. 这个表可以申请几张卡？

💻 TASK 4. E-MAIL

You've just returned from opening up your first account in a Chinese bank, and you want to tell a friend about the experience. E-mail your friend and describe the services that your bank offers. Were you there to deposit money? Into which account did you deposit your money? Can you use the ATM machines? Why or why not? Did you apply for a credit card? What kind and why? Remember to use the grammar and vocabulary from this lesson!

32

定火车票
Taking the Train

 听力练习 (Tīnglì Liànxí)
Listening Exercises

 TASK 1. BINGO

In this section, you will hear various Chinese phrases and sentences. Demonstrate your understanding of them by numbering their English counterparts in the order in which you hear them.

A. Phrases

to reserve a ticket online

to have a long weekend

to be very satisfied

which day to set out?

too pessimistic

top bunk or bottom (in a sleeper car)?

to admire your scenic photo

schedule on the wall

soft seat or hard seat

one round-trip ticket

ticket office at a train station

good news

tourist guidebook

to make travel plans

to be a tour guide

to visit famous historical sites

B. Sentences

They keep placing my train schedule everywhere these past few days. I don't know where it is now.

If I travel by train, I will neither buy a hard seat nor a soft seat. I will only buy a sleeping berth.

It is not convenient to get up and down when sleeping on the top bunk.

The hard seats on the train are certainly cheaper, but (you) cannot sleep in them.

They are going to buy two round-trip tickets from Beijing to Xi'an.

When they return to Beijing, do they want to go by soft sleeper or hard sleeper?

She wants to take some pictures of the scenery in Xi'an and send them to her parents.

We are about to leave. Did you bring the map?

Today he brought me a tourist guidebook of Xi'an.

🎧💻 TASK 2. SHORT CONVERSATIONS

Listen to the short conversations. Select the correct answer for each question from the choices provided.

1. 是/不是
2. 火车上/售票处
3. 今天/明天
4. 男的/女的
5. 在/不在

🎧💻 TASK 3. MONOLOGUE

Listen to the two passages and answer the questions below.

Passage 1

Supplementary Vocabulary

躺   tǎng   *v.*   to lie down

Questions

1. What is this woman talking about?

    a) what kind of train ticket she bought for her trip

    b) what kind of train tickets are the most expensive

    c) what kind of train ticket she likes the most

    d) none of the above

2. Which berth in the train does the woman like best?

    a) the lower level

    b) the upper level

    c) the middle level

    d) none of the above

Passage 2

Questions

1. What is this man talking about?

   a) where his teacher wants to go during the break

   b) where his friend does not want to go during the break

   c) where he could possibly go during the break

   d) none of the above

2. Which of the following statements is correct?

   a) The man and his friend want to visit Shanghai together.

   b) The man and his teacher want to visit Xi'an together.

   c) The man wants to visit Shanghai instead of Xi'an.

   d) The man wants to visit Xi'an instead of Shanghai.

🎧💻 TASK 4. DIALOGUE

Listen to the dialogue and answer the questions below.

1. What is this conversation about?

   a) The woman is inviting the man to visit her.

   b) The man is inviting the woman to visit him.

   c) The man and the woman are planning a trip together.

   d) None of the above.

2. Who pays for the ticket?

   a) the man

   b) the woman

   c) both the man and the woman

   d) neither one

3. What is the relationship between the two speakers?

   a) husband and wife

   b) a ticket agent and a customer

   c) a tour guide and a customer

   d) two friends

4. How long are the man and the woman going to be together?

    a) one day

    b) two days

    c) three days

    d) four days

口语练习 (Kǒuyǔ Liànxí)
Speaking Exercises

 TASK 1. SUBSTITUTION

Familiarize yourself with basic sentence patterns by substituting the given phrases into the following sentences.

1. A: 喂，你现在在哪儿？

   B: 我在（售票处门口）。你（过来）吧。

饭馆里边	进来
教室外边	出来
楼下	下来
楼上	上来

2. A: 你的（室友）上哪儿去了？

   B: 他（上楼）去了。

姐姐	上街
哥哥	下楼
朋友	进教室
老师	上北京

3. A: 你给我（带）来了一些什么东西？

   B: 我给你（带）来了一些（茶）。

借　　　　　　　书

拿　　　　　　　点心

送　　　　　　　礼物

寄　　　　　　　咖啡

买　　　　　　　水果

4. A: 你们出去玩儿了半天，怎么样啊？

　　B: 我们玩儿得很好，既（学了本领），又（见了世面）。

聊了天　　　　　学了中文

看了电影　　　　交了新朋友

骑了自行车　　　锻炼了身体

唱了歌　　　　　跳了舞

5. 他既不（会上网预订火车票），也不（会打电话预订）。

想当医生　　　　想当护士

愿意搞生意　　　愿意搞电脑

喜欢喝咖啡　　　喜欢喝茶

知道那个人的名字　知道那个人的地址

6. （好）是（好），可是（太旧了）。

大　　　　　　　穿上很舒服

方便　　　　　　太贵了

便宜　　　　　　质量不好

7. （好）是（好），可是（我们去哪儿呢）？

愿意　　　　　　谁带我们去呢

有时间　　　　　我们怎么去呢

想看书　　　　　我们看什么呢

🎧💻 TASK 2. QUICK RESPONSE

The following exercise will challenge your listening and speaking abilities and help you to develop good conversational skills.

A. Answering Questions

Listen to the following questions and provide an answer to each one. If you don't know a word, try to guess its meaning from the context, rather than looking it up. Remember, both speed and accuracy are important!

1. 你今年放假打算上哪儿去？为什么？

2. 你为什么总想出去旅游？

3. 要是你去北京，你想不想找一个导游？为什么？

4. 如果你有机会去中国，你最想到哪儿去参观？为什么？

B. Asking Questions

Listen to the following statements and follow the hints in the right-hand column to ask a related question for each statement. Try to avoid using the 吗-type question.

	Hints
1. 我想买两张从北京去西安的火车票。	（几张）
2. 我当然可以当导游。你看我有旅游指南还有地图。	（怎么能）
3. 长途太累。麻烦您给我一张硬卧吧。	（什么）
4. 我喜欢下铺，不过上铺也行。	（还是）

🎧💻 TASK 3. GUIDED ROLE-PLAYING

Listen to the following dialogues between two native speakers. Select Role A or Role B and have a dialogue with the computer. After familiarizing yourself with the conversation, construct and record your own dialogue by replacing as many words as possible with related terms. Be creative, but be careful not to disrupt the structure of the conversation!

1. Making Travel Plans

   A: 放假以后咱们去旅游吧。

   B: 好啊。我一直想去北京逛一逛。那儿的名胜古迹可多了！

   A: 北京的风景也非常漂亮。我们去北京既能见世面，又能学语言。太棒了。

   B: 一言为定。我来给咱们当导游。我一会儿就去买旅游指南和北京地图。

A: 我去给咱们买火车票。我们什么时候走？什么时候回来？

B: 周末到外地去的火车票很不好买。我们下个星期一早上走吧。

2. Buying a Train Ticket

A: 麻烦你给我买两张从西安去北京的来回火车票。

B: 你想要哪天的？准备什么时候从北京回来？

A: 下个星期二早上走，星期四晚上回来。

B: 你可以坐 K 83 次特快，早上 8:50 出发，晚上 10:30 到。您要买什么票？

A: 给我两张软卧。我们想上了火车就睡觉。你有没有下铺？

B: 对不起，没有下铺了。只有上铺，你要不要？

TASK 4. PICTURE DESCRIPTION

Describe the pictures using the grammar and the vocabulary you learned in this lesson. Use your imagination!

读写练习(Dú Xiě Liànxí)
Reading/Writing Exercises

 TASK 1. SHORT STORY

Read the story and answer the questions that follow.

成语故事：井底之蛙

很久很久以前，在一个快干枯的井里，有一只青蛙。这只青蛙从小到大没有到井的外边去玩儿过。所以，他不知道井的外面是什么样子。他每天能看见的天也只有井口那么大。一天，一个海龟到井口边来玩儿。青蛙跟海龟吹牛说："你看，我在井里多么快乐啊。我可以在井底跑来跑去，在水里游来游去，真是舒服极了。你也下来玩玩儿吧"。海龟刚要下去，就害怕了。因为井里边又黑又小。他对青蛙说："你上来吧。我们到大海的边上去玩儿，好吗"？青蛙问："什么是大海"？海龟说："你没见过大海吗？大海是蓝色的水，又大又深，可漂亮了"。"海能比天大？比我的井还深吗"？青蛙好奇地问。海龟回答说："海虽然没有天大，可比你的井深啦。住在大海里才是真正的快乐呢"。青蛙听了以后，得意地对海龟说："可是天也才跟我的井口一样大"。海龟听了青蛙话，很长时间都不知道应该说什么。他觉得青蛙真的应该出去见见世面了。

Supplementary Vocabulary

1. 井底之蛙 jǐng dǐ zhī wā   *phr.*   (lit.) frog in a well; a narrow-minded, inexperienced, or shortsighted person

   井   *n.*   well
   底   *p.w.*   bottom
   之   *part.* 的
   （青）蛙   *n.*   frog

2. 干枯   gānkū   *adj.*   dry

3. 只   zhī   *m.w.*   measure word for animals

4. 井口   jǐngkǒu   *n.*   opening of a well

5. 海龟　　hǎiguī　　　　　*n.*　　　turtle

6. 大海　　dà hǎi　　　　　*n.*　　　sea, ocean

7. 得意　　déyì　　　　　　*adj.*　　self-satisfied, complacent, pleased with oneself

Questions

1. 青蛙住在井里，既快乐又舒服。　　　　True/False

2. 青蛙快乐是快乐，可是不是真正的快乐。　True/False

3. 青蛙比海龟见世面见得多。　　　　　　　True/False

4. 海龟很羡慕青蛙的日子。　　　　　　　　True/False

 ## TASK 2. CHENGYU STORY

Read the 成语故事 below and answer the following questions.

塞翁失马

很久很久以前，有一个很聪明的老人，大家都叫他塞翁。塞翁跟他儿子住在一起。家里还有一匹马。塞翁非常喜欢他那匹马。每天都带他的马出去玩儿。有一天，塞翁的马跑丢了，大家都为他伤心。可是塞翁说："没事。这件事说不定会变成一件好事儿呢"？过了几天，那匹马不但自己跑回来了，而且还带回来了一匹又高又大的好马。大家赶快跑来为塞翁庆祝。塞翁对大家说："你们都觉得我的马自己回来了，还带回来了一匹好马。这一定是一件好事。但是我们不要高兴得太早了。这种好事也有可能变成一件坏事儿"。几个星期以后，塞翁的儿子因为骑马，摔断了腿。塞翁对他儿子说："你别伤心。坏事儿有时候会变成一件好事儿。你应该乐观一点儿"。过了一年多，战争开始了。很多男人都得去打仗，可是塞翁的儿子因为腿摔断了，不能去参加打仗，所以一直没有离开过塞翁。

Supplementary Vocabulary

1. 失　　　shī　　　　　*v.*　　　　　to lose

2. 匹　　　pǐ　　　　　　*m.w.*　　　measure word for a horse

3. 摔断　　shuāi duàn　　*v. comp.*　to fall and break something

4. 战争   zhànzhēng   *n.*   war

5. 打仗   dǎ zhàng   *v. obj.*   to go to war, to fight

Proper Nouns

塞翁   Sàiwēng   the old man who lives near the border

Questions

1. 塞翁失马是什么意思？

2. 看完这个故事，你觉得塞翁聪明不聪明？为什么？

3. 在你的生活里，你认识像塞翁这样的人吗？讲一讲他的故事。

💻 TASK 3. AUTHENTIC MATERIAL

In this section, you will be exposed to some authentic materials that people use in China. Look at the receipts and answer the following questions.

#1

#2

Questions

1. 这三张都是什么票？

2. 哪张票最贵？

3. 从北京到西安的票是哪种座位的？

4. 请你说一说火车的班次和出发时间。

💻 TASK 4. E-MAIL

E-mail your friend and ask him/her to visit a famous scenic spot in Beijing with you this weekend. To convince your friend, you provide a list of reasons explaining why you want to go. Be sure to tell your friend why you feel that way.

33

风味小吃

A Taste of China

 听力练习(Tīnglì Liànxí)

Listening Exercises

 TASK 1. BINGO

In this section, you will hear various Chinese phrases and sentences. Demonstrate your understanding of them by numbering their English counterparts in the order in which you hear them.

A. Phrases

a restaurant that serves local specialties

to take a look at the menu

local specialties

sweet, sour, bitter, hot, and salty

famous dishes

a bowl of steaming soy milk

to add sugar and salt

to have no empty seats

to order a favorite dish

the price list on the wall

don't like it too salty

to match his taste

authentic taste

leftover dishes

no need to leave a tip

to smell something delicious

B. Sentences

Why are you pacing back and forth?

The minute I walked in, I started to get hungry. Let's order some food!

The service at this restaurant is so good; no wonder they have so much business.

Please bring me that dish, and you can take this dish away.

When they walked into the restaurant, they saw lots of other customers.

There were no empty seats downstairs, so the waiter took them upstairs.

These few dishes are all famous local specialties.

The restaurant that serves good native food is not very far. We can cut across from here.

We ordered too many dishes, and my stomach feels like it's going to burst!

🎧💻 TASK 2. SHORT CONVERSATIONS

Listen to the short conversations. Select the correct answer for each question from the choices provided.

1. 喜欢／不喜欢
2. 好／不好
3. 有／没有
4. 是／不是
5. 一个人／两个人

🎧💻 TASK 3. MONOLOGUE

Listen to the two passages and answer the questions below.

Passage 1

1. What is the woman talking about?

    a) The woman wants to open a 小吃店 in America.

    b) The woman now knows how to make soy milk and fried pancakes herself.

    c) The woman wants to take some fried pancakes with her to America.

    d) The woman believes that the food in the 小吃店 would sell well in America.

2. Which of the following statements is correct?

    a) The woman is in China when she delivers this speech.

    b) The woman frequently goes to the 小吃店 to have breakfast.

    c) The woman likes soy milk and fried pancakes.

    d) None of the above.

Passage 2

1. What is this man talking about?

    a) The man wants to open a 小吃店 with good customer service.

    b) The man has a 小吃店 with very good business.

    c) The man talks about how his 小吃店 should attract more customers.

    d) None of the above.

2. Which one of the following statements is NOT correct?

   a) The customers like this 小吃店.

   b) The customers in this 小吃店 do not need menus.

   c) The customers know what each 小吃 looks like before they order.

   d) None of the above.

🎧📖 TASK 4. DIALOGUE

Listen to the dialogue and answer the questions below.

1. What is the conversation about?

   a) The woman is trying to get some information about 小吃店.

   b) The man is trying to get some information about 小吃店.

   c) Both of them are trying to get some information about 小吃店.

   d) None of the above.

2. What's the relationship between the man and the woman?

   a) two friends

   b) two strangers

   c) girlfriend and boyfriend

   d) husband and wife

3. Which of the following statements is correct?

   a) The woman wants to know whether each 小吃 has its own name.

   b) The woman has to order her dishes from a waiter.

   c) Customers eat first and pay afterwards.

   d) None of the above.

4. Which of the following statements is correct?

   a) The 小吃店 is not too far away and is easy to find.

   b) The 小吃店 is far away but is easy to find.

   c) The 小吃店 is not far away but is difficult to find.

   d) The 小吃店 is far away and also difficult to find.

口语练习(Kǒuyǔ Liànxí)

Speaking Exercises

 TASK 1. SUBSTITUTION

Familiarize yourself with basic sentence patterns by substituting the given phrases into the following sentences.

1. A: 他从(外地)(带回来)了什么东西？

   B: 他(带回来)了(一个随身听)。

楼上	送下来	一个电脑
外边	搬进来	几把椅子
楼下	拿上去	两瓶酒
对面	送过来	一些小吃
学校	寄出去	一个包裹

2. A: (那些点心)你(送过去)了吗？

   B: 我还没(送过去)呢！

这本地图	带回去
那两张画	挂上去
那个存款单	收起来
他寄来的信	找出来

3. A: (我的室友)呢？

   B: 你看，(你的室友)从(咖啡馆里)(走出来)了。

服务员	厨房里	走过来
看电影的人	电影院	跑出去
胡老师	前边	穿过马路去
他的女朋友	南门	跑进去
老王的车	停车场	开出来

4. 我一(走进来)就(觉得饿)了。

收到护照　　去办签证

不舒服　　　去看病

看见电梯　　不想走楼梯

拿到火车票　离开西安

5. A: 老师一(进教室来)，学生就怎么样了？

　　B: 学生就(站起来)了。

说下课　　　跑出去了

发作业　　　高兴地拿过去做

讲完语法　　开始问问题

问问题　　　开始紧张

🎧💻 TASK 2. QUICK RESPONSE

The following exercise will challenge your listening and pronunciation abilities and help you to develop good conversational skills.

A. Answering Questions

Listen to the following questions and provide an answer to each one. If you don't know a word, try to guess its meaning from the context, rather than looking it up. Remember, both speed and accuracy are important!

1. 欢迎你们到我们的小吃店。想来一点什么？

2. 你最喜欢吃什么口味(or 地方风味)的菜？为什么？

3. 你喜欢在饭馆吃饭还是在小吃店吃饭？为什么？

4. 你点菜的时候，不知道点什么，你应该怎么问服务员？

B. Asking Questions

Listen to the following statements and follow the hints in the right-hand column to ask a related question for each statement. Try to avoid using the 吗-type question.

Hints

1. 我们这儿没有菜单。墙上挂着价格表。（有没有）

2. 你给我来一碗羊肉泡馍吧。　　　　　　（什么）

3. 豆浆请不要加糖，我不喜欢吃甜的。　（加不加）

4. 我们这儿的油饼最有名气。　　　　　　（什么）

🎧💻 TASK 3. GUIDED ROLE-PLAYING

Listen to the following dialogues between two native speakers. Then select Role A or Role B and have a dialogue with the computer. After familiarizing yourself with the conversation, construct and record your own dialogue by replacing as many words as possible with related terms. Be creative, but be careful not to disrupt the structure of the conversation!

1. Ordering Food

    A: 请问，您想来点儿什么？

    B: 你们这儿什么菜有名？你给我推荐几个菜吧。

    A: 我们这儿鸡肉饼非常有名，味道纯正，要不要尝尝？

    B: 我想吃一点儿素的。

    A: 我们这儿的油饼不错。是用素油炸的。

    B: 好吧，给我一个油饼，再来一碗豆浆。

    A: 请稍等，我一会儿就给您送过来。

2. Asking to Take Food Home

    A: 我们这儿的菜怎么样？喜欢不喜欢吃？

    B: 喜欢。味道又香又纯正。

    A: 您还要点儿别的吗？我们这儿的甜点不错。

    B: 不吃了。我吃得太撑了。这个荤菜，请你帮我打一下包，我想带回去。

    A: 请您等一下，我一打好包，就给您送过来。

TASK 4. PICTURE DESCRIPTION

Describe the pictures using the grammar and the vocabulary you learned in this lesson. Use your imagination!

 读写练习 (Dú Xiě Liànxí)
Reading/Writing Exercises

 TASK 1. SHORT STORY

Read the story and answer the True/False questions that follow.

李丽莉和吴文德听说大华饭馆是一家很有名的北方风味儿的饭馆儿。一天晚上，他们俩儿到那儿去吃晚饭。他们一走进大门，吴文德就往中间的一张大桌子走了过去，他刚刚坐下来，一位服务员就走了过来对他说：两位吗？请跟我到楼上去吧。

李丽莉小声地对吴文德说："吴文德，这是饭馆，不是小吃店。不能自己找座位。"吴文德说："怪不得那个服务员不让我坐在那张大桌子旁边。"他们两个人在二楼坐下来以后，服务员拿过来两本菜单，很客气地说：请先看菜单。李丽莉说："吴文德，你先点一个你最喜欢吃的菜。"吴文德看了看菜单，问服务员："你们的鸡做得怎么样？"服务员回答说："炸鸡是我们厨师的拿手菜，又新鲜又好吃。"吴文德说："那我就尝一尝你们做的炸鸡吧。"李丽莉点了一个素菜，又要一碗面条。过了一会儿，服务员端着一碗热腾腾的面条走过来问："这碗面是哪位的？"李丽莉指着吴文德说："是他的。"吴文德奇怪地问："我点了一个炸鸡，你为什么还要给我点面条呢？"李丽莉笑着回答说："今天是你的生日。过生日应该吃面条。"吴文德觉得更奇怪了：过生日为什么要吃面条？李丽莉耐心地说："过生日吃面条是中国的文化。面条很长，代表着长寿。祝你生日快乐！"吴文德高兴地说："你真够朋友。我以为你早就忘了今天是我的生日了呢。"李丽莉说："怎么会忘记呢？你今年二十二岁。我明年跟你同岁。"

Supplementary Vocabulary

1.	小声	xiǎoshēng	*adj.*	in a low voice
2.	新鲜	xīnxiān	*adj.*	fresh
3.	端	duān	*v.*	to carry
4.	面条	miàntiáo	*n.*	noodles
5.	奇怪	qíguài	*adj.*	strange
6.	长寿	chángshòu	*n.*	long life
7.	同岁	tóngsuì	*phr.*	the same age

Questions

1. 因为那天是吴文德的生日，所以李丽莉请他去饭馆吃饭。

    True/False

2. 李丽莉和吴文德一走进饭馆，就上二楼往一张大桌子走过去。

    True/False

3. 服务员的服务很周到，给他们推荐了厨师的拿手菜炸鸡。

True/False

4. 中国人过生日的时候，要吃荤菜和面条，可以活得很久很健康。

True/False

TASK 2. CULTURAL KNOWLEDGE

After reading the passage, use your own words to write your responses to the questions below.

中国人多地大。住在不同地方的人吃东西的口味也不一样。很多人都知道，住在中国南方的人一般都爱吃甜的，住在北方的人爱吃咸的，四川人喜欢吃辣的，山西人喜欢吃酸的。因为每个地方的饭、菜都有自己的风味，所以，慢慢地就有了很多不同风味的地方菜或地方小吃。中国很多地方都有自己著名的代表菜。例如：

省	风味	代表菜	
四川菜	麻、辣、酸	麻婆豆腐	(mápó dòufu, Mapo Tofu)
江苏菜	甜、咸	上海小排	(Shànghǎi xiǎopái, Shanghai Ribs)
湖南菜	酸、辣、香、鲜	麻辣子鸡	(málà zǐjī, Hot Pepper Chicken)
陕西小吃	咸、香、鲜	羊肉泡馍	(yángròu pàomó, bread soaked in mutton soup)

很多城市也有自己的一些著名菜。例如：北京的北京烤鸭 (kǎoyā, Roast Duck) 已经有三百多年的历史了；天津的狗不理包子 (gǒu bùlǐ bāozi, "steamed dumplings that the dog does not pay attention to") 西安的饺子宴有上百年的历史。有机会去中国，别忘了尝尝这些菜。

Supplementary Vocabulary

1.	不同	bùtóng	*adj.*	different
2.	南方	nánfāng	*n.*	southern region
3.	北方	běifāng	*n.*	northern region
4.	省	shěng	*n.*	province
5.	麻	má	*adj.*	(feeling) a prickling sensation
6.	城市	chéngshì	*n.*	city
7.	历史	lìshǐ	*n.*	history

Proper Nouns

1. 江苏   Jiāngsū   a province in China

2. 湖南   Húnán   a province in China

3. 山西   Shānxī   a province in China

Questions

1. 这些地方的风味菜，你吃过哪些？你说说他们的味道怎么样。

2. 请你谈谈在你们国家里有些什么著名的代表菜。

💻 TASK 2. AUTHENTIC MATERIAL

The following is a menu from a restaurant in China. Look at the menu and answer the following questions.

Menu from a Sichuan-style snack shop located in Xi'an.

Questions

1. 这个饭店卖哪个地方风味的菜？
2. 在"炒菜"里哪个菜跟小吃的价钱差不多？
3. 要是你只有 10 块钱，你会点什么？
4. 要是你有 50 块钱你会点什么？

TASK 4. E-MAIL

After eating at a Chinese 小吃店, you e-mail your friend to tell him/her about the experience. Write a paragraph or two telling your friend what 小吃店 is and how it is different from a regular restaurant. Tell your friend what you ate and describe how it tasted.

34

住旅馆

Staying in a Hotel

 听力练习(Tīnglì Liànxí)

Listening Exercises

 TASK 1. BINGO

In this section, you will hear various Chinese phrases and sentences. Demonstrate your understanding of them by numbering their English counterparts in the order in which you hear them.

A. Phrases

to stay in a single room

to put down a deposit

to give me an explanation

do not drink

to reach the standard

too late to visit

these soft drinks

hotel registration desk/place

to return everything

never stayed in a hotel before

driver's license

checking the meter

the key to the room

so expensive (that it is scary)

purified water or tap water

to plan to check out

B. Sentences

Now I remember, he was the driver who took us the long way around.

I can't recall the address of the hotel right now.

Those drinks are so expensive! Don't drink them.

It looks like we won't have enough time to visit the famous historical sites.

He doesn't sound like a hotel employee who would work at the registration desk.

Don't worry. If we don't break anything, they will return our deposit.

It's lucky that you brought the key; otherwise, how would we get back into the room?

She never explained the matter to me.

Let's check out tomorrow. I can't stay in this hotel any longer.

🎧💻 TASK 2. SHORT CONVERSATIONS

Listen to the short conversations. Select the correct answer for each question from the choices provided.

1. 女的/男的
2. 知道/不知道
3. 是/不是
4. 会/不会
5. 喝了/没喝

🎧💻 TASK 3. MONOLOGUE

Listen to the two passages and answer the questions below.

Passage 1

1. What is this woman talking about?

   a) why she currently lives in a hotel

   b) why she wants to live in a hotel

   c) why she does not like to stay in hotels

   d) none of the above

2. Which one of the following is correct?

   a) The woman thinks that checking into the hotel is time-consuming.

   b) The woman thinks that cleaning is too time-consuming.

   c) The woman wants to stay in the hotel as long as possible.

   d) All of the above.

Passage 2

Supplementary Vocabulary

招待所   zhāodàisuǒ   *n.*   guesthouse

Questions

1. What is this man talking about?

   a) how he does not like to drink tea

   b) how he started drinking tea

   c) how he drinks tea all day long

   d) none of the above

2. Which one of the following is correct?

    a) The man likes drinking cold beverages.

    b) The man does not like Chinese beverages.

    c) The man has been drinking tea since last year.

    d) All of the above.

🎧💻 TASK 4. DIALOGUE

Listen to the dialogue and answer the questions below.

1. What are the man and the woman talking about?

    a) The woman wants to check in to a hotel.

    b) The woman wants to check out of a hotel.

    c) The man wants to check in to a hotel.

    d) The man wants to check out of a hotel.

2. Where does the conversation take place?

    a) in the hotel guest room

    b) outside the hotel

    c) in the lobby of the hotel

    d) none of the above

3. Which of the following is NOT correct?

    a) The guest has enjoyed her stay in the hotel.

    b) The hotel employee is willing to give the guest a larger room.

    c) The guest thinks that the drinks in her room are complimentary.

    d) The guest wants to check out.

4. What happens at the end of the conversation?

    a) The guest gets her deposit back.

    b) The guest does not get back any of her deposit.

    c) The guest gets back some of her deposit.

    d) None of the above.

口语练习 (Kǒuyǔ Liànxí)
Speaking Exercises

 TASK 1. SUBSTITUTION

Familiarize yourself with basic sentence patterns by substituting the given phrases into the following sentences.

1. 他们一(谈起话)来，就要(谈)几个小时。

唱起歌	唱
跳起舞	跳
吃起饭	吃
喝起茶	喝

2. (这些登记手续)办起来很(麻烦)。

这件事	做	容易
那种茶	闻	香
这本书	看	有意思
那条裤子	穿	不舒服

3. 我(想)出来了(一个好主意)。

写	一本书
做	一个好菜
炸	一个油饼
看	你们没住过旅馆
听	你们是中国人
闻	你做的是中国饭

4. (这家旅馆)我(住)不下去了。

这个故事	讲
这条新闻	听

那么难的数学课　　学

这么难吃的药　　　吃

这么多的水　　　　喝

5. 我（说）得（都不想再说了）。

　　看　　　　　　　　高兴极了

　　忙　　　　　　　　没时间睡觉

　　累　　　　　　　　饭都不想吃了

6. A:（中文语法），你（学得会学不会）？

　　B:（学）得（会）。

　　那本书　　　　　　　找得到找不到　　　找　　　　到

　　今天的作业　　　　　做得完做不完　　　做　　　　完

　　这些单词　　　　　　记得住记不住　　　记　　　　住

　　我给你发的电子邮件　收得到收不到　　　收　　　　到

　　这个随身听　　　　　修得好修不好　　　修　　　　好

7. A: 我在（宾馆里边）等你，你（进得来）吗？

　　B: 我（进不去）。

　　上边　　　　　　　　上得来　　　　　　上不去

　　张老师那儿　　　　　去得了　　　　　　去不了

　　家里　　　　　　　　走得回来　　　　　走不回去

　　学校停车场　　　　　开得进来　　　　　开不进去

🎧💻 TASK 2. QUICK RESPONSE

The following exercise will challenge your listening and speaking abilities and help you to develop good conversational skills.

A. *Answering Questions*

Listen to the following questions and provide an answer to each one. If you don't know a word, try to guess its meaning from the context, rather than looking it up. Remember, both speed and accuracy are important!

1. 在中国，住旅馆都需要办什么手续？

2. 在中国住旅馆，你退房的时候能拿回你的押金吗？为什么？

3. 你要是住在中国的旅馆，你会不会喝你房间的饮料？为什么？

4. 要是你的出租汽车司机带着你兜圈子，你应该怎么办？

B. *Asking Questions*

Listen to the following statements and follow the hints in the right-hand column to ask a related question for each statement. Try to avoid using the 吗-type question.

Hints

1. 我找得到那个小吃店。   （找得到，找不到）

2. 这条路我们开得进去。   （吗）

3. 他的执照号码我抄下来了。   （了没有）

4. 我想出来了一个好主意。   （什么）

🎧💻 TASK 3. GUIDED ROLE-PLAYING

Listen to the following dialogues between two native speakers. Then select Role A or Role B and have a dialogue with the computer. After familiarizing yourself with the conversation, construct and record your own dialogue by replacing as many words as possible with related terms. Be creative, but be careful not to disrupt the structure of the conversation!

1. Checking In at a Hotel

   A: 请问，你这儿今天晚上有房间吗？

   B: 请稍等，我查一下。你打算住几个晚上？

   A: 就今天晚上，明天早上我就退房。

   B: 今天晚上我们这儿有一个空的单人间。您带证件了吗？

   A: 带了。单人间多少钱一晚上？

   B: 八十九块一晚上，还要交 100 块钱押金。一共一百八十九块。

   A: 你这儿刷卡吗？

   B: 刷。……这是您房间的钥匙，有问题请给我们前台打电话。

2. Checking Out of a Hotel

A: 你好。麻烦你给我办一下儿退房手续。

B: 您住多少号房间？您房间的钥匙呢？

A: 这是我的钥匙。我住一〇四号房间。

B: 请稍等，我们的服务员已经去房间检查了。

A: 我昨天晚上打了一个长途电话，不知道多少钱？

B: 长途电话是三十二块人民币。您交了 100 块钱押金，找您六十八块。

A: 谢谢。

B: 欢迎您再来。

TASK 4. PICTURE DESCRIPTION

Describe the pictures using the grammar and the vocabulary you learned in this lesson. Use your imagination!

读写练习(Dú Xiě Liànxí)
Reading/Writing Exercises

 TASK 1. SHORT STORY

Read the story and answer the questions that follow.

旅馆

如果你到中国去学习或者去工作，你不用自己去找旅馆，很多大学都有自己的宾馆。这些宾馆一般要比外边的旅馆便宜。如果你去中国旅游参观，你也不用担心找旅馆的事儿。你下了飞机以后，很多旅馆都派代表去机场接飞机。这些代表每个人手里都拿着一个大牌子，牌子上写着旅馆的名字，每个代表还带着很多小册子，给你介绍旅馆的情况，价格，离机场有多远，等等。你千万不要急着定旅馆，你应该花几分钟的时间，仔仔细细地研究一下儿每个旅馆的情况，然后再选一个旅馆。有一些旅馆还有免费从机场到旅馆接送客人的班车。

去中国旅游你还可以找旅行社帮忙。旅行社会帮助你安排住的地方。旅行社给你安排的旅馆一般要比你自己找的好，价格也会比你自己找的旅馆便宜。你如果有语言困难，很多中国的高中生或者大学生都能说一些英语，而且他们非常喜欢和外国人说英语，也非常愿意帮忙。所以你不要不好意思，放心地问谁会说英语。你一定能找到一个愿意而且能给你帮忙的人。祝你去中国旅游顺利。

Supplementary Vocabulary

1. 派	pài	v.	to send
2. 小册子	xiǎo cèzi	n.	pamphlet, brochure
3. 情况	qíngkuàng	n.	situation, circumstances
4. 免费	miǎnfèi	adj.	free of charge
5. 班车	bānchē	n.	shuttle (bus)
5. 旅行社	lǚxíngshè	n.	travel agency
6. 安排	ānpái	v.	to arrange

Questions

1. 看起来到中国去旅游，找旅馆的事不是一个大问题。

　　　　　　　　　　　　　　　　　　　　　　True/False

2. 旅行社常常会派代表去机场帮助旅客安排旅馆的事。

　　　　　　　　　　　　　　　　　　　　　　True/False

3. 一般中国人都听得懂英文，愿意帮外国游客。

　　　　　　　　　　　　　　　　　　　　　　True/False

4. 如果你是外国留学生，可以在自己大学的宾馆住下来，
不用找旅馆。　　　　　　　　　　　　　　　True/False

 TASK 2. CHENGYU STORY

Read the 成语故事 below and answer the following questions.

班门弄斧

很久很久以前，一个非常有名的木匠，他的名字叫鲁班。鲁班用木头做出来的东西漂亮极了。大家都很佩服他的技术。从来没有人的技术能比鲁班好。有一天，有一个木匠，走到一个大红门的房子前面，他不知道那就是鲁班的家。他对大家说："我的木匠技术非常好，因为我是跟鲁班学的木匠。我用我这个斧头能做出又好看又实用的东西来"。旁边的人指着他对面的大红门问："你能做出比这个大红门更好的门吗？"这个木匠说："我这个人从来不吹牛。我做的大门一定比这个大红门要好得多。"旁边的人听了，大笑了起来。一个人对这个木匠说："那就是鲁班的家，那个大门就是鲁班自己做的。你能做出比这个大红门更好的门吗？"这个木匠听说自己是在鲁班家的大门前面吹牛，就马上不好意思地走开了。

Supplementary Vocabulary

1. 班门弄斧	Bān mén nòng fǔ	*phr.*	(lit.) to show off with an axe in front of Lu Ban's door; to show off one's meager skills before an expert; 鲁班 (Lu Ban) is the name of a famous architect.
班			
门		*n.*	door
弄		*v.*	to wield, to handle
斧		*n.*	axe

2. 木匠	mùjiang	*n.*	carpenter
3. 木头	mùtou	*n.*	wood, timber
4. 佩服	pèifu	*v.*	to admire
5. 技术	jìshù	*n.*	skills
6. 实用	shíyòng	*adj.*	practical

Questions

1. 为什么这个木匠会觉得不好意思？
2. 在什么情况，可以用"班门弄斧"这个成语？你能不能说几个例子？

🖥 TASK 3. AUTHENTIC MATERIAL

In this section, you will be exposed to some authentic materials that people use in China. Look at the rate chart of a hotel and answer the following questions.

空港花园酒店

客房价目表

客房种类	房价
豪华套房	RMB1280
标准间	RMB 480
三人间	RMB 580

以上价格另加北京城市建设费6.00元
人民币/人/晚

* 酒店退房时间为正午12时正

* 十二岁以下一名儿童可免费与父母同住

* 可接受信用卡：美国运通卡，大来卡，万事
  达卡，VISA卡，JBC卡，长城卡，牡丹卡

* 房价如有变动恕不另行通知

订 房 联 系
中国·北京首都国际机场

电话：(010) 64566351

传真：(010) 64562991

邮编：100621

Questions

1. 这家旅馆有几种房间？
2. 这家旅馆退房的时间是几点？
3. 这家旅馆接受几种信用卡？
4. 在飞机场能不能订这家旅馆的房间？

 TASK 4. E-MAIL

You have just checked into your hotel room and discovered that the room has an Internet connection! E-mail your friends, telling them all about the hotel. Where are you staying, and how long will you be there? Does the hotel have a swimming pool? Are you planning to order room service later? Maybe the hotel is a little run-down, and you feel uncomfortable staying there. Tell your friends all about it, and remember to use the grammar and vocabulary from this lesson!

35

锻炼身体
Keep Fit!

 听力练习(Tīnglì Liànxí)
Listening Exercises

 TASK 1. BINGO

In this section, you will hear various Chinese phrases and sentences. Demonstrate your understanding of them by numbering their English counterparts in the order in which you hear them.

A. Phrases

to have a sports meet

from elementary to intermediate class

to suddenly have stage fright

to cheer friends on

to take a picture of a radio announcer

to win first place

to applaud the athletes

ever since (he) twisted (his) ankle

high score in the competition

taiji performance

to break a record

to meet at the east side of the sports ground

win or lose?

all the spectators

to run, to swim, and to play basketball

no self-confidence

B. Sentences

Where did she start playing basketball?

It was two months ago that I broke the school's record.

It was such a bad timing that my ankle suddenly got twisted.

He is here to cheer the athletes on, not to attend the competition.

Could you take a picture of me and the radio announcer?

The runners participating in the competition will be entering the field very soon.

She is the one who got a high score. She transferred from the elementary to the intermediate class last week.

She had stage fright when she was performing.

Since he won the provincial sports meet, his self-confidence has been growing and growing.

🎧💻 TASK 2. SHORT CONVERSATIONS

Listen to the short conversations. Select the correct answer for each question from the choices provided.

1. 在学校/在省里
2. 男的/女的
3. 两个/三个
4. 对/不对
5. 会/不会

🎧💻 TASK 3. MONOLOGUE

Listen to the two passages and answer the questions below.

Passage 1

1. What is the man talking about?

   a) He is explaining why he is still doing taijiquan.

   b) He is explaining why he gave up taijiquan.

   c) He is explaining why he does not do taijiquan at all.

   d) None of the above.

2. Which of the following is NOT correct?

   a) The man thought it was difficult for him to learn taijiquan.

   b) The man is eager to show off his taijiquan.

   c) The man's teacher has great confidence in his ability to do taijiquan.

   d) The man did not volunteer to perform at the sports meet.

Passage 2

1. What is the woman talking about?

   a) She is deciding whether to participate in the sports meet.

   b) She intends to break the school record at this sports meet.

   c) The spectators are all getting excited at the sports meet.

   d) None of the above.

2. Which of the following is correct?

    a) The narrator thinks that the spectators should participate in the competition.

    b) The narrator still holds the school's long distance record so far.

    c) The woman thinks the athletes are not working hard enough.

    d) None of the above.

🎧📖 TASK 4. DIALOGUE

Listen to the dialogue and answer the questions below.

1. What is this conversation about?

    a) The woman does not want to give up jogging.

    b) The man does not want to give up jogging.

    c) The woman does not want the man to give up jogging.

    d) The man does not want the woman to give up jogging.

2. Why did the woman start playing basketball?

    a) She has friends who like playing basketball.

    b) She is not very good at other sports.

    c) The man wants her to play basketball with him.

    d) None of the above.

3. Who holds the school running record?

    a) the man

    b) the woman

    c) the man and the woman

    d) neither of them

4. Which of the following is correct?

    a) The woman wants to keep jogging and playing basketball.

    b) The woman only wants to keep jogging.

    c) The woman only wants to play basketball.

    d) None of the above.

口语练习(Kǒuyǔ Liànxí)
Speaking Exercises

 TASK 1. SUBSTITUTION

Familiarize yourself with basic sentence patterns by substituting the given phrases into the following sentences.

1. A: （箱子）那么（大）！你（搬）得动，（搬）不动？

   B: 没问题，我（搬）得动。

路	远	走
车	旧	开
东西	重	拿
山	高	爬

2. A: （今天的游泳比赛）你（去）得了（去）不了？

   B: 我（去）得了，你放心吧。

明天的生日晚会	来
那些东西	用
这么多菜	吃
这些钱	花

3. A: （操场上）（站）得下那么多的（运动员）吗？

   B: 我不知道（站）得下（站）不下。

房间里	住	客人
学校里	停	车
教室里	坐	学生
公共汽车里	挤	乘客

4. 你们昨天是怎么去(运动会)的？

我们是(走)去的。

看电影	开车
图书馆	骑自行车
银行	坐公共汽车
邮局	打的
宿舍	跑

5. 你是在(美国)长大的吗？

我不是在(美国)长大的，我是在(中国)长大的。

法国	英国
英国	日本
日本	德国
德国	美国

6. (宿舍外边)的那个人是来干什么的？

他是来(找我)的。

楼下	修电脑
门口	送信
教室里边	问问题
出租车旁边	参加晚会

7. 他自从(打篮球)以后，就更(喜欢跑步)了。

生病	注意锻炼身体
学中文	想去中国
得了第一名	喜欢游泳
有了借记卡	不爱带现金

🎧💻 TASK 2. QUICK RESPONSE

The following exercise will challenge your listening and pronunciation abilities and help you to develop good conversational skills.

A. Answering Questions

Listen to the following questions and provide an answer to each one. If you don't know a word, try to guess its meaning from the context, rather than looking it up. Remember, both speed and accuracy are important!

1. 你喜欢锻炼吗？为什么？
2. 你最喜欢做什么运动？
3. 你喜欢看什么比赛？为什么？
4. 你参加过什么运动比赛？赢了还是输了？

B. Asking Questions

Listen to the following statements and follow the hints in the right-hand column. Use the 是⋯的 structure to ask a related question for each statement. Try to avoid using the 吗-type question.

	Hints
1. 我两年前开始打篮球。	（什么时候）
2. 我在中国学的太极拳。	（在哪儿）
3. 我昨天跟我朋友去看游泳比赛。	（跟谁）
4. 广播员叫所有的运动员都到操场东边去集合。	（谁）

🎧💻 TASK 3. GUIDED ROLE-PLAYING

Listen to the following dialogues between two native speakers. Select Role A or Role B and have a dialogue with the computer. After familiarizing yourself with the conversation, construct and record your own dialogue by replacing as many words as possible with related terms. Be creative, but be careful not to disrupt the structure of the conversation!

1. Talking about a Basketball Game

A: 昨天晚上的篮球比赛，你看了吗？

B: 没有看。谁跟谁比？

A: 是我们学校跟你们学校比赛。

B: 谁赢了？

A: 当然是我们学校赢了。

B: 幸亏我没去看。

2. Talking about Sports

A: 我听说你今年又打破省里的游泳记录了。

B: 是谁告诉你的？

A: 我哥哥。他说你游泳的成绩非常好。你真棒！

B: 哪里。哪里。我今年练习得比较多。你喜欢什么运动？

A: 我喜欢跑步，也喜欢打篮球。你想不想跟我比赛、比赛？

B: 免了，免了。我一定会输的。我一点儿也跑不动。

TASK 4. PICTURE DESCRIPTION

Describe the pictures using the grammar and the vocabulary you learned in this lesson. Use your imagination!

读写练习(Dú Xiě Liànxí)
Reading/Writing Exercises

 TASK 1. SHORT STORY

Read the story and answer the questions that follow.

我叫林小业，是北京语言文化大学的学生。我哥哥是北京大学的学生。今天我们学校跟北京大学比赛篮球，我跟我哥哥都去了。但是我们不是去打球的，我们是去当观众的。我们两个学校打得都很好，想打赢一场比赛很难。上次是我们赢的，但是那天的比赛是在我们学校打的。今天我们在他们那儿打，还能不能赢呢？观众早就到了。很多是从我们这两个大学来的，他们都是来给自己学校的篮球运动员加油的。但是，也有一些是从其他的学校来看球赛的。

球赛就要开始了。我看得出来我们的队员都有一点儿紧张。但是我们今天一定会比上次打得更好，因为我们篮球队来了一位新队员。你看，就是那个高高的。他叫张明。他虽然跑步跑得不太快，但是个子特别高，比别的队员高出一个头来。他是这个学期才从上海来的。我听说他从上中学以后，就开始打篮球。他的初中学校和高中学校都是因为有了他，所以常常得第一名。现在他到我们这儿来了，我们也一定能拿第一。

Supplementary Vocabulary

其他   qítā   *adj.*   other

Questions

1. 我们学校跟北京大学一共有几次比赛？
   a) 一次
   b) 两次
   c) 三次
   d) 四次

2. 上次这两个学校比赛篮球，哪个学校赢了？

　　a) 北京大学

　　b) 北京语言文化大学

　　c) 不知道

　　d) a) + b) + c) 都不对

3. 这次篮球比赛是在哪儿比的？

　　a) 北京大学

　　b) 北京语言文化大学

　　c) 在其他学校

　　d) a) + b) + c) 都不对

4. 林小业为什么觉得他的学校这次一定赢得了？

　　a) 因为他学校的篮球队员比以前棒。

　　b) 因为他学校的观众比北京大学的观众多。

　　c) 因为他学校的篮球队员不那么紧张。

　　d) a) + b) + c) 都不对

📖 TASK 2. CHENGYU STORY

Read the 成语故事 below and answer the following questions.

自相矛盾

矛和盾是古时候常用的两种兵器。矛是一种刺杀的兵器；盾是一种保护自己的兵器。有一天，有一个贩子到街上去卖矛和盾。他想多赚一点儿钱，所以他对旁边看热闹的人说："你们看看我的这个矛，多锐利啊。这个矛什么东西都可以刺穿，可好用了。大家快来买吧。"过了一会儿这个贩子看没有人买他的矛，就从地上拿起一个盾，对大家说："我的这个盾质量非常好，什么矛都刺不穿"。有一个好奇的人，拿起这个贩子的矛和盾，问那个贩子说："请问，要是我用你的矛来刺你的盾。到底是你的矛厉害，还是你的盾厉害"。那个贩子想了半天，不知道应该怎么回答，只好拿着自己的矛和盾走开了。

Supplementary Vocabulary

1.	自相矛盾	zìxiāng máodùn	*phr.*	be self-contradictory
	自			self
	相		*adv.*	mutual, reciprocal
	矛		*n.*	spear
	盾		*n.*	shield
2.	古	gǔ	*adj.*	ancient
3.	兵器	bīngqì	*n.*	weapons
4.	刺杀	cìshā	*v.*	to stab
5.	保护	bǎohù	*v.*	to protect
6.	锐利	ruìlì	*adj.*	sharp
7.	刺穿	cìchuān	*v.comp.*	to stab through
8.	只好	zhǐhǎo	*adv.*	have to, can't help but

Questions

1. 你觉得这个小贩会不会卖东西？为什么？

2. 你能说一个"自相矛盾"的例子吗？

📔 TASK 3. AUTHENTIC MATERIAL

Read the announcement of a sports meet and answer the following questions.

西安外院 第五十六届 田径运动会

时间：二〇〇四年 四月十日 - 四月十二日
开幕式：学院操场，四月十日上午9:00-10:00

欢迎光临

闭幕式：
四月十二日
16:00-17:00

项目		男子比赛时间	女子比赛时间
100米短跑	预赛	4/10, 13:00-14:00	4/10, 14:15-15:15
	决赛	4/11, 12:00-13:00	4/11, 13:15-14:15
200米短跑	预赛	4/10, 15:30-16:30	4/10, 16:45-17:45
	决赛	4/10, 14:30-15:30	4/11, 15:45-16:45
1500米中长跑	预赛	4/11, 09:00-10:00	4/11, 10:15-11:15
	决赛	4/12, 09:00-10:00	4/12, 10:15-11:15
3000米长跑	预赛	4/11, 14:00-17:00	4/11, 14:00-17:00
	决赛	4/12, 14:00-17:00	4/12, 14:00-17:00
4X100米接力	预赛	4/10, 14:00-17:00	4/10, 14:00-17:00
	决赛	4/11, 14:00-17:00	4/11, 14:00-17:00
跨栏	预赛	4/11, 14:00-17:00	4/11, 14:00-17:00
	决赛	4/12, 14:00-17:00	4/12, 14:00-17:00
跳高	预赛	4/11, 13:00-15:00	4/11, 13:00-15:00
	决赛	4/12, 13:00-15:00	4/12, 13:00-15:00
跳远	预赛	4/10, 10:00-12:00	4/10, 14:00-16:00
	决赛	4/11, 10:00-12:00	4/11, 14:00-16:00
铅饼	预赛	4/10, 16:00-19:00	4/10, 12:00-15:00
	决赛	4/11, 16:00-19:00	4/11, 12:00-15:00
铅球	预赛	4/11, 16:00-19:00	4/11, 12:00-15:00
	决赛	4/12, 16:00-19:00	4/12, 12:00-15:00

1. 这个运动会是在哪儿举行的？
2. 这个运动会举行了多少天？
3. 这个运动会有多少项目？
4. 选出你最喜欢的三个比赛项目的时间和地点。

 TASK 4. WEB SURFING

Use <<yahoo.com.cn>> or any other web site to find a sports event and write a summary of that event. What was the event? Did your team win or lose? If you prefer, you may also talk about an athlete you admire. Use the "是…的"structure to help your friend get a vivid picture of the experience.

36
我生病了
I Don't Feel Well...

 听力练习 (Tīnglì Liànxí)
Listening Exercises

 TASK 1. BINGO

In this section, you will hear various Chinese phrases and sentences. Demonstrate your understanding of them by numbering their English counterparts in the order in which you hear them.

A. Phrases

to have a high fever

to take one's body temperature

to have a bad cough

to have a sore throat

to have a severe headache

to have a flu

to go to a pharmacy to pick up medicine

to take medicine on time

to pick up your number from the hospital registration office

to go to the hospital to see an internal specialist

to recover from an illness

to give her a number for emergency treatment

to have a blood test

to give her an injection

to be hospitalized for treatment

to still have a fever

B. Sentences

(If you) want to recover quickly, you must take the medicine on time.

As soon as I got busy, I forgot all about getting a doctor's excuse.

You have to go to the registration office to get a number for internal medicine.

He got the flu and his whole body ran out of energy. Now he is lying down and resting.

Luckily he brought in a clinical thermometer, otherwise, how could we take his temperature?

I had my blood work done, had an X ray, then went to the pharmacy to get the medicine.

His throat is red and swollen, and he also has a chest pain. Let's take him to the emergency room.

He got a lung disease and it is contagious. He has to be hospitalized for treatment.

You should take the medicine for bringing down the fever three times a day, one tablet each time, on an empty stomach.

🎧💻 TTASK 2. SHORT CONVERSATIONS

Listen to the short conversations. Select the correct answer for each question from the choices provided.

1. 厉害/不厉害
2. 应该/不应该
3. 男的/女的
4. 吃了/没有
5. 是/不是

🎧💻 TASK 3. MONOLOGUE

Listen to the two passages and answer the questions below.

Passage 1

1. What is this woman talking about?

   a) She took her roommate to see a doctor.

   b) Her roommate took her to see a doctor.

   c) Both she and her roommate got sick.

   d) None of the above.

2. Which one of the following is NOT correct?

   a) The patient's illness got worse.

   b) The patient's illness got better.

   c) The patient did not take the medicine on time.

   d) The patient had a fever and a cough.

Passage 2

1. What is the narrator's profession?

   a) He is a teacher.

   b) He is a doctor.

   c) He is a nurse.

   d) He is a patient.

2. In addition to cough medicine, how many pills does the patient have to take?

    a) a total of two pills per day

    b) a total of four pills per day

    c) a total of six pills per day

    d) none of the above

🎧📖 TASK 4. DIALOGUE

Listen to the dialogue and answer the questions below.

1. What are the two speakers talking about?

    a) symptoms of the illness

    b) duration of the illness

    c) instructions for taking medication

    d) all of the above

2. What is the relationship between the two speakers?

    a) two friends

    b) doctor and nurse

    c) doctor and patient

    d) doctor and patient's friend

3. Which of the following is NOT correct?

    a) The patient has a fever.

    b) The patient is very sick.

    c) The patient's illness is not very serious.

    d) The patient is hospitalized.

4. Which of the following is correct?

    a) The patient does not have any fever.

    b) The patient has to get an injection.

    c) The patient has to take six pills a day.

    d) None of the above.

口语练习 (Kǒuyǔ Liànxí)

Speaking Exercises

 TASK 1. SUBSTITUTION

Familiarize yourself with basic sentence patterns by substituting the given phrases into the following sentences.

1. A: (你)把(住院手续办完)了没有?

   B: 还没呢。

他	电视打开
吴文德	单词记住
你哥哥	自行车修好
你妹妹	练习做完
你姐姐	大衣穿上

2. A: 他把(病人)(送到)哪儿了?

   B: (送到)(急诊室去)了。

车	停在	停车场
照片	挂在	客厅的墙上
药	放到	床边的桌子上
刚写的信	寄到	中国去
我新买的衣服	收在	箱子里

3. A: 他把(那些药)给(病人)(送去)了吗?

   B: 都(送去)了。

| 那几张照片 | 你妈妈 | 拿来 |
| 那些书 | 你朋友 | 还回去 |

那些点心　　你爷爷　　带来

那几条裙子　你姐姐　　寄去

4. 今天你不(吃药)不行。你赶快把(药)(吃)了。

喝水　　　　　水　　　　　喝

做作业　　　　作业　　　　做

读报纸　　　　报纸　　　　读

复习单词　　　单词　　　　复习

5. 你今天不能不(量体温)。你现在就把(体温量一量)吧！

洗衬衫　　　　这件衬衫洗一洗

检查作业　　　这个作业检查一遍

念课文　　　　课文念几遍

量血压　　　　血压量一下儿

关窗户　　　　窗户关一下儿

开门　　　　　门开一下儿

6. 他非要把(这件事)(告诉他朋友)不可。

这本书　　　　送给我

那几只笔　　　放在桌子上

客人　　　　　送到车站去

我们的故事　　写成小说

🎧💻 TASK 2. QUICK RESPONSE

The following exercise will challenge your listening and speaking abilities and help you to develop good conversational skills.

A. Answering Questions

Listen to the following questions and provide an answer to each one. If you don't know a word, try to guess its meaning from the context, rather than looking it up. Remember, both speed and accuracy are important!

1. 你觉得哪儿不舒服？是不是感冒了？

2. 医生给你开了一些什么药？怎么吃？一天几次，一次几片？

3. 生病的时候你愿意打针还是吃药？为什么？

4. 你生病的时候你跟医生要假条吗？为什么？

B. Asking Questions

Listen to the following statements and follow the hints in the right-hand column to ask a related question for each statement. Try to avoid using the 吗-type question.

Hints

1. 我头疼得厉害，还咳嗽。   （哪儿）

2. 这个药一天三次，每次一片。饭前半小时吃。   （怎么）

3. 我以为我得了流感了，但是医生说是感冒。   （什么）

4. 我把今天的药吃完了。   （了没有）

🎧💻 TASK 3. GUIDED ROLE-PLAYING

Listen to the following dialogues between two native speakers. Then select Role A or Role B and have a dialogue with the computer. After familiarizing yourself with the conversation, construct and record your own dialogue by replacing as many words as possible with related terms. Be creative, but be careful not to disrupt the structure of the conversation!

1. Seeing a Doctor

   A: 医生，我头疼、嗓子疼。

   B: 你在发高烧。你把嘴张开，我看看你的嗓子。你还觉得哪儿不舒服？

   A: 胸也疼、还咳嗽。

   B: 嗓子有点红肿。你感冒了，先叫护士给你打退烧针。

   A: 我以为我得了什么大病呢。

   B: 没事。我给你开点儿药。回去把药吃了，休息两天就好了。

2. Taking Medicine

   A: 你已经吃了三天药了，好一点儿了吗？

   B: 还是有点发烧。咳嗽咳得也很厉害。

A: 退烧的药每天三次，每次一片。空腹吃。你按时吃药了吗？

B: 吃了。但是我只吃了一天。烧一退，我就再没吃了。

A: 咳嗽糖浆你吃了几次？

B: 我吃了两次。早晚各一次，每次一勺。第二天，就停药了。

TASK 4. PICTURE DESCRIPTION

Describe the pictures using the grammar and the vocabulary you learned in this lesson. Use your imagination!

读写练习 (Dú Xiě Liànxí)
Reading/Writing Exercises

 TASK 1. CHENGYU STORY

Read the 成语故事 below and answer the following questions.

对症下药

华佗是中国古代最著名的医生。因为他看病的技术好极了，所以大家都叫他神医。有一次，有两个人一起到华佗那儿去看病，两个人都是头痛发烧。但是，华佗给这两个人看了病以后，给两个人开了两种不同的药。这两个人取了药以后，觉得很奇怪，就去问华佗为什么他们两个人得的是一种病，但是吃的药不一样。华佗笑着对他们两个人说：你们俩的病看起来是一样的，但是你们得病的原因不一样。你们一个人是因为吃东西不合适引起了头痛发烧，另一个人是因为感冒引起的头痛发烧。所以，给你们两个人治病的方法也不一样。两个人回家以后，把华佗给他们开的药都吃了。很快两个人的病就都好了。

Supplementary Vocabulary

1. 对症下药	duìzhèng xiàyào	*phr.*	suit the medicine to the illness, act appropriately for the situation
对		*prep.*	according to, vis-à-vis
症		*n.*	ailment
下		*v.*	to determine, to prescribe
药		*n.*	medicine
2. 华佗	Huà Tuó	*n.*	name of a famous doctor in ancient China
3. 神医	shényī	*n.*	magical doctor
4. 原因	yuányīn	*n.*	reason
5. 引起	yǐnqǐ	*v.*	to cause

Questions

1. 为什么大家都把华佗叫作 "神医"？
2. 你能不能想出几种困难的情况，再找出"对症下药"的方法？

TASK 2. COMPREHENSIVE FILL-IN

Read the following passage and write down the words that are missing. If you need help, please refer to your Multimedia CD-ROM.

我在中国住了二十多年，在美国也住了二十多年。当然，在中国，在美国我都看过病。在中国看病和在美国看病有很多不一样的地方，最不一样的就是在美国看病要预约。就是你感冒发(1)，咳(2)头疼，也得先预约才能去看病。在中国，病人不能预约。病人直接去医院，到医院的挂号(3)挂号。等轮到自己的号码的时候，病人(4)能看病。但是最近几年，中国也有几家非常好的医院也开始预约了。

病人在中国做检查的时候，也不用预约。如果需要化验、透视等，也都不用预(5)，这些检查室都在医院里。拿着化验单或透视单去排(6)，就行了。等排到你了，你就把透视单交(7)放射科的医生就能透视。还有，拿药的时候，要在(8)的窗口前排队取药。总之，在中国的医院里，你又可以看病，又可以做检(9)，还可以做治疗。在美国就不一样了，要是大夫觉得你应该透视，就会给你开个透视(10)。但是你不能马上去透视。你要和透视的地方预约，在约定的时间去透视。一样的地方是中国和美国的急(11)病人都不用预约，可以把病人直接送(12)急诊室检查。

Supplementary Vocabulary

1. 放射科	fàngshè kē	*n.*	radiology department
2. 总之	zǒngzhī	*adv.*	in sum
3. 约定	yuēdìng	*v.*	to agree on

TASK 3. AUTHENTIC MATERIAL

In this section, you will be exposed to some authentic materials used in China. Look at the forms used in a hospital and answer the following questions.

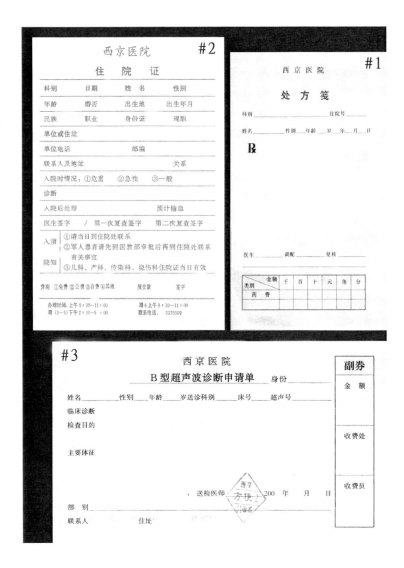

Questions

1. 哪张要交钱？

2. 医生说病人得做 B 超，病人应该用哪张？

3. 看完病以后要拿药，应该用哪张？

4. 如果病人病得很重，不能回家，需要用哪个？

💻 TASK 4. E-MAIL

Your roommate has been very sick for two days, and you finally took him to see a doctor. He is in the hospital now, and you are e-mailing his mother to let her know his condition. The content of your e-mail should include the following:

1. His illness.

2. The doctor's diagnosis and proposed treatments.

3. Directions for taking medication.

37

过春节

Happy Chinese New Year!

 听力练习(Tīnglì Liànxí)
Listening Exercises

 TASK 1. BINGO

In this section, you will hear various Chinese phrases and sentences. Demonstrate your understanding of them by numbering their English counterparts in the order in which you hear them.

A. Phrases

within ten days

to add to the holiday atmosphere

each and every family

at daybreak

to wish children happiness

New Year's wishes

to be interested in local customs and traditions

to paste spring couplets

to get close to something exciting

to be swept very clean

to visit each other at home

to send a short message

to celebrate Spring Festival

to pay a New Year's visit

to set off firecrackers everywhere

loud voice

B. Sentences

Is the New Year's dinner ready yet?

No matter how hard he cleans the room, it is still not very clean.

As far as we are concerned, you may introduce China's customs anytime.

During Spring Festival, I am most interested in setting off firecrackers.

During Spring Festival, she doesn't do any work.

The Spring Festival couplet still has not been pasted on the door.

It turned out that none of those guests knew how to wrap dumplings.

Every place is crowded during Chinese Spring Festival.

No matter which year it is, his family always hangs two red lanterns.

🎧💻 TASK 2. SHORT CONVERSATIONS

Listen to the short conversations. Select the correct answer for each question from the choices provided.

1. 好看/不好看
2. 贴了/没贴
3. 有人/没有人
4. 好买/不好买
5. 敢/不敢

🎧💻 TASK 3. MONOLOGUE

Listen to the two passages and answer the questions below.

Passage 1

1. Which of the following is correct?

   a) The New Year's party takes place on New Year's Day.

   b) The man knows something about traditional Chinese customs.

   c) This year the Chinese New Year comes before the start of school.

   d) All of the above.

2. Which of the following is NOT correct?

   a) The New Year's party is for Chinese students who cannot go home.

   b) The New Year's party is by invitation only.

   c) Anyone who wants to attend the party is welcome.

   d) All of the above.

Passage 2

1. What is this woman talking about?

   a) She is too busy to make preparations for the Chinese New Year.

   b) She is going to celebrate Chinese New Year with her family.

   c) She is not going to celebrate Chinese New Year.

   d) She is going to celebrate Chinese New Year by herself.

2. Which of the following is correct?

    a) The woman's friend asks the woman to bring gifts for everyone.

    b) The woman's friend wants to bring some gifts for everyone.

    c) Everyone, except her, seems to have time to prepare for Chinese New Year.

    d) None of the above.

🎧💻 TASK 4. DIALOGUE

Listen to the dialogue and answer the questions below.

1. What are the two speakers talking about?

    a) whether they should go to visit her parents

    b) what time the store closes

    c) whether they should buy a gift for her parents

    d) what gift they should buy for her parents

2. When does this conversation take place?

    a) in the morning

    b) in the afternoon

    c) in the evening

    d) at night

3. Which of the following is correct?

    a) The couple is going to the man's parents' home for the New Year.

    b) The couple is going to the woman's parents' home for the New Year.

    c) The couple is inviting the man's parents over for the New Year.

    d) The couple is inviting the woman's parents over for the New Year.

4. Which of the following is correct?

    a) The man comes up with some ideas, but the woman does not agree.

    b) The woman comes up with some ideas, but the man does not agree.

    c) The man agrees with the woman's ideas.

    d) The woman agrees with the man's ideas.

口语练习(Kǒuyǔ Liànxí)
Speaking Exercises

 TASK 1. SUBSTITUTION

Familiarize yourself with basic sentence patterns by substituting the given phrases into the following sentences.

1. （饺子）（包好）了吗？

　　（饺子）已经（包好）了。

　　（饺子）还没有（包好）。

年夜饭	摆在桌子上
银行的手续	办完
随身听	买到
咖啡	煮好
茶	泡好

2. （饺子）（包）得太多了，我们怎么（吃）也（吃）不完。

作业	给	做
鞭炮	买	放
饭	做	吃
咖啡	煮	喝
单词	教	记

3. 我家这个月谁都（忙），什么（年货）都没（买）。

紧张	灯笼	挂
累	春联	贴
不舒服	地方	去
没精神	电影	看

4. 你们(什么时候)去(放鞭炮)都可以。

    什么时间   逛街

    下午几点   做练习

    哪天上午   外语系

    哪个星期   办签证

5. 今天你们在哪个(教室学习)都(没问题)。

    饭馆吃饭   会觉得香

    阅览室读报纸   可以

    咖啡馆喝咖啡   会满意

    商店买东西   可以退换

    舞场跳舞   不花钱

6. (过年)的时候，他们一边(包饺子)，一边(看电视)。

    周末   打扫房子   收拾东西

    开晚会   唱歌   跳舞

    工作   用电脑   打电话

    晚上在家   聊天   做饭

7. 原来我对(过节)很感兴趣，现在我只对(放鞭炮)感兴趣。

    打篮球   跑步

    参观名胜古迹   地方小吃

    天气预报   每天的气温

    听音乐   跳舞

8. 怪不得他(那么开心)原来他(一个星期之内过了两个节)。

    没去游泳   病了

    要去参加比赛   跑步跑得很快

    不想住旅馆   觉得旅馆不干净

    出门不带现金   有一张信用卡

    很会讲价钱   常去夜市讨价还价

🎧💻 TASK 2. QUICK RESPONSE

The following exercise will challenge your listening and speaking abilities and help you to develop good conversational skills.

A. Answering Questions

Listen to the following questions and provide an answer to each one. If you don't know a word, try to guess its meaning from the context, rather than looking it up. Remember, both speed and accuracy are important!

1. 除夕是什么意思？
2. 拜年是什么意思？
3. 在中国你去朋友家拜年的时候应该说什么？
4. 你每年新年都在哪儿过？怎么过？

B. Asking Questions

Listen to the following statements and follow the hints in the right-hand column to ask a related question for each statement. Try to avoid using the 吗-type question.

<table>
<tr><td></td><td></td><td>**Hints**</td></tr>
<tr><td>1.</td><td>中国人过年的时候又贴春联又挂灯笼，还放鞭炮。</td><td>（什么）</td></tr>
<tr><td>2.</td><td>我们在美国过年和中国人在中国过年过得不太一样。</td><td>（一样不一样）</td></tr>
<tr><td>3.</td><td>我明年要去中国过个春节。</td><td>（为什么）</td></tr>
<tr><td>4.</td><td>除夕那天晚上大家一边聊天，一边吃东西，
一直要闹到天亮。</td><td>（怎么）</td></tr>
</table>

🎧💻 TASK 3. GUIDED ROLE-PLAYING

Listen to the following dialogues between two native speakers. Select Role A or Role B and have a dialogue with the computer. After familiarizing yourself with the conversation, construct and record your own dialogue by replacing as many words as possible with related terms. Be creative, but be careful not to disrupt the structure of the conversation!

1. How Was Your Spring Festival?

   A: 你今年春节过得怎么样？

   B: 很过瘾。我想什么时候吃饭，就什么时候吃饭。我想什么时候睡觉，就什么时候睡觉。舒服极了。

   A: 哪儿都是鞭炮声，你怎么能睡得着觉呢？

   B: 我睡觉的时候，什么声音都听不见。你呢？春节过得好不好？

   A: 我从来都不喜欢过春节。火车上，商店里，街上哪儿都那么挤。谁都那么忙。

   B: 你过节的时候，你应该什么也看不见。想怎么放松就怎么放松。

2. Comparing Chinese New Year with Christmas

   A: 中国的春节真热闹，家家户户都贴春联放鞭炮。

   B: 就像美国人过圣诞节的时候家家户户都挂彩灯一样。

   A: 春节早上，中国人见面都说"过年好"。

   B: 圣诞节早上美国人见面都说"圣诞快乐"。

   A: 中国人除夕全家人在一起包饺子吃年夜饭。

   B: 美国人圣诞夜也是全家人在一起吃饭。

Supplementary Vocabulary

| 圣诞节 | Shèngdànjié | Christmas |
| 彩灯 | cǎidēng | decorated lights |

TASK 4. PICTURE DESCRIPTION

Describe the pictures using the grammar and the vocabulary you learned in this lesson. Use your imagination!

  读写练习(Dú Xiě Liànxí)

Reading/Writing Exercises

TASK 1. SHORT STORY

Read the story and answer the True/False questions that follow.

"年"的故事

我小的时候听我爷爷讲过一个"年"的故事。我爷爷说，很久很久以前，山里有一只大老虎，人们把它叫作"年"。每年冬天，"年"饿了的时候，在山里找不到吃的东西，就要下山来吃人。所以大家都非常怕"年"。一听到有人喊"年来了！"，人们就都跑走了。每年冬天，"年"都把大家吓得睡不好觉，吃不下饭。大家都快急死了。

一天，有一个很聪明的老人想出来了一个好主意。因为"年"非常喜欢吃穿旧衣服的人。他叫每个人都准备一件新衣服，每家都做一些好吃的东西。等"年"来的时候，大家谁都把新衣服穿上，把好吃的东西放在外边给"年"吃。"年"吃饱了，就不吃人了。后来，人们又发明了鞭炮。过年的时候，人们不停地放鞭炮，把"年"吓得再也不敢下山来吃人了。很多年过去了，这就慢慢地变成了一个习惯。新年到了，人们都穿新衣服、做好吃的、放鞭炮。当然，现在我们说的过年的那个"年"，已经不是那个时候的"年"了。现在过年，人们都是互相串门、打电话、或发手机短信来拜年，祝新年好。每个人都希望自己和自己的家人、自己的朋友能一年比一年过得好。

Supplementary Vocabulary

1. 山   shān   *n.*   mountain

2. 老虎   lǎohǔ   *n.*   tiger

3. 它   tā   *pron.*   it

4. 喊   hǎn   *v.*   to cry out

5. 发明   fāmíng   *v.*   to invent

Questions

1. 老虎每年冬天下山吃人。所以大家把它叫作"年"。   True/False

2. 老虎饿了的时候，什么都不想吃只想吃人。   True/False

3. 放鞭炮是老人想出来的好主意，要把老虎吓跑。   True/False

4. 现在人们过年的时候可以用很多种方法拜年。   True/False

🖋 TASK 2. CULTURAL KNOWLEDGE

After reading the passage, use your own words to write your responses to the questions below.

春节是中国农历的新年，很多人经常会问什么是农历？中国的农历有平年和闰年。平年有十二个月，六个大月，六个小月。大月有三十天，小月有二十九天，全年一共三百五十四天。这样，每三年就少了三十三天，所以每三年就要加一个月。有十三个月的那年就叫做闰年，那第十三个月就叫做闰月。农历的新年也就是正月初一。正月是农历每年的第一个月，初一是农历每月的第一天。农历的每月一号到十号也叫作"初一、初二……初十"。因为农历的正月是春天的开始，所以大家又把农历的新年叫做春节。

Supplementary Vocabulary

1. 农历   nónglì   *n.*   the lunar calendar
2. 平年   píngnián   *n.*   a lunar year with twelve months
3. 闰年   rùnnián   *n.*   a lunar year with thirteen months
4. 正月初一   zhēngyuè chūyī   *phr.*   January 1 in the lunar year

Questions

用你自己的话说一说、写一写什么是农历？什么是中国 的春节？

 ## TASK 3. CHENGYU STORY

Read the 成语故事 below and answer the following questions.

滥竽充数

古代的时候，有一位国王很喜欢听人吹竽。那个时候的竽很像现在的笛子。国王一共有三百多人给他吹竽。他每次听人吹竽的时候，总是叫这三百多个人一起给他吹。每个吹竽的人都能挣很多钱。

有一位名字叫南郭的先生，一点儿也不会吹竽，但是他很羡慕那些吹竽的人，因为他们挣钱比他挣得多。一天，南郭先生见到国王的时候，他告诉国王他很会吹竽，国王听了很高兴，就叫南郭先生跟其他的人一起去吹竽。后来，每次国王要听竽，南郭先生就混在其他吹竽的人里面，假装吹竽。因为吹竽的人很多，谁也没有注意到南郭先生不会吹竽。

有一天，国王死了。他的儿子当了国王。这个新国王也喜欢听人吹竽。但是他不喜欢让大家在一起吹竽。他每次听人吹竽的时候，都叫那些人一个一个地给他吹。南郭先生看了就知道自己不能再假装吹竽，所以就跑走了。

Supplementary Vocabulary

1. 滥竽充数	lànyú chōngshù	*phr.*	(lit.) to pretend to play the *yu* and be a member of the band; make up one of the number, contribute no work in a group but be undetected because of the work of others
滥		*b.f.*	excessive, indiscriminate
竽		*n.*	flute
充		*b.f.*	to fill
数		*n.*	number
2. 古代	gǔdài	*n.*	ancient times
3. 笛子	dízi	*n.*	flute
4. 国王	guówáng	*n.*	king
5. 后来	hòulái	*adv.*	afterwards, later
6. 混	hùn	*v.*	to mix, to muddle

Questions

1. 请用你自己的话来说一说滥竽充数是什么意思？
2. 对你来说，南郭先生是一个什么样的人？
3. 你见过"滥竽充数"这样的事情吗？请你讲一讲。

💻 TASK 4. E-MAIL

E-mail your friend and tell him/her how you celebrated Christmas Eve last year. Include descriptions of activities for both children and adults, and any preparations you made for Christmas Eve and/or Christmas Day dinner.

38
打工
Making Some Pocket Money

 听力练习 (Tīnglì Liànxí)
Listening Exercises

 TASK 1. BINGO

In this section, you will hear various Chinese phrases and sentences. Demonstrate your understanding of them by numbering their English counterparts in the order in which you hear them.

A. Phrases

summer job

to make some pocket money

student's parents

advertisement on a bulletin board

a temporary position

to be invited to China

to meet at the publisher's office

to print out

to turn on the air conditioner

to consider study very important

to attend a preparatory class

your responsibilities

my work unit

want ad

to like dealing with people

to make a copy

B. Sentences

After you print your résumé please make a copy for me.

Let's divide our responsibilities. Searching for jobs online will be your responsibility.

Since last summer, I have gotten a job and started making some pocket money.

He was invited by the publisher to do some translation work.

The want ads on the bulletin board have been torn down by others.

If we apply too late, the jobs will be taken by others.

As a matter of fact, (you can) learn a lot from the math preparatory class in the summer.

I hope I will be able to teach in the future so I can be called "Zhang Laoshi" by my students.

You see my face is covered with sweat. My fan was borrowed by someone else.

🎧💻 TASK 2. SHORT CONVERSATIONS

Listen to the short conversations. Select the correct answer for each question from the choices provided.

1. 有了/没有
2. 女的/男的
3. 在/不在
4. 想/不想

🎧💻 TASK 3. MONOLOGUE

Listen to the two passages and answer the questions below.

Passage 1

Questions

1. What is this woman talking about?

    a) She wants to focus on her studies.

    b) She has decided not to study, but to work.

    c) She has decided to find a job while studying.

    d) None of the above.

2. Which of the following is correct?

    a) The woman did some translation work at the beginning of the semester.

    b) The woman has good translation skills.

    c) The woman has found a translation job.

    d) None of the above.

Passage 2

Supplementary Vocabulary

挑选   tiāoxuǎn   *v.*   to pick, to select

Questions

1. What is this man talking about?

    a) The man wants to get a summer job.

    b) The man's friend wants to get a summer job.

    c) Both the man and his friend want to get summer jobs.

    d) Neither one wants a summer job.

2. Which of the following is correct?

   a) The bulletin board at school has postings for summer jobs.

   b) There are many opportunities for summer jobs.

   c) The speaker has not gotten any job yet.

   d) All of the above.

🎧💻 TASK 4. DIALOGUE

Listen to the dialogue and answer the questions below.

1. What is the primary focus of this conversation?

   a) the man's job

   b) the woman's job

   c) both of their jobs

   d) none of the above

2. Who has a job now?

   a) the man

   b) the woman

   c) both the man and the woman

   d) neither one

3. Which of the following is correct?

   a) The man is more picky about his job than the woman.

   b) The woman is more picky about her job than the man.

   c) Both of them are picky about their jobs.

   d) Neither one is picky about their job.

4. Which of the following is NOT correct?

   a) The man only wants to do computer jobs.

   b) The man does not want to do computer jobs.

   c) The man wants to work with people.

   d) None of the above.

口语练习 (Kǒuyǔ Liànxí)
Speaking Exercises

 TASK 1. SUBSTITUTION

Familiarize yourself with basic sentence patterns by substituting the given phrases into the following sentences.

1. (布告栏上的招聘广告) 都叫/让人 (撕光) 了。

那几本小说	借走
单人间	占
学校的游泳记录	打破
图书馆的电脑	用坏

2. (这本小说) 被她 (翻译成) (英文) 了。

寄件人	写成	收件人
地铁站	当成	汽车站
打工挣零花钱	看作	一件大事
她的室友	叫作	大翻译家

3. 他被 (邀请) 到 (饭馆) 去 (吃饭) 了。

送	医院	看病
叫	老师办公室	开会
请	中国	搞研究
聘	出版社	搞翻译

4. (办补习班的事) 由我负责，(贴广告的事) 由你负责，怎么样？

打开水	泡茶
存钱	取钱
填包裹单	汇款
挑样式	讨价还价

5. 我以为他(有暑期临时工作了)，其实他(还在找)。

是来参加比赛的	是来给运动员加油的
必须要打针	吃药就行了
喜欢吃甜的	只喜欢吃辣的
只带了现金	还带了一个借记卡

6. 很多人从(高中)起就开始(打工挣零花钱)。

小学	用电脑
中学	学中文
大学	谈对象
研究生	写书

🎧💻 TASK 2. QUICK RESPONSE

The following exercise will challenge your listening and speaking abilities and help you to develop good conversational skills.

A. Answering Questions

Listen to the following questions and provide an answer to each one. If you don't know a word, try to guess its meaning from the context, rather than looking it up. Remember, both speed and accuracy are important!

1. 你暑假打工吗？为什么？
2. 你父母鼓励你去打工挣钱吗？为什么？
3. 你喜欢找什么临时工作？为什么？
4. 要是你想在中国找一个临时的工作，你应该上哪儿去找？怎么找？

B. Asking Questions

Listen to the following statements and follow the hints in the right-hand column to ask a related question for each statement. Try to avoid using the 吗-type question.

	Hints
1. 我如果教英文，就会被学生叫作吴老师。	（谁）
2. 我暑假想找临时工作，挣点儿钱。	（为什么）
3. 我从高中起就开始打工挣零花钱。	（什么时候）
4. 布告栏上的招聘广告都快让人撕光了。	（什么东西）

🎧💻 TASK 3. GUIDED ROLE-PLAYING

Listen to the following dialogues between two native speakers. Then select Role A or Role B and have a dialogue with the computer. After familiarizing yourself with the conversation, construct and record your own dialogue by replacing as many words as possible with related terms. Be creative, but be careful not to disrupt the structure of the conversation!

1. Talking about Summer Plans

   A: 就要放暑假了，你们有什么计划？

   B: 我们想找个临时工作，挣点儿零花钱。

   A: 你想找什么工作呢？

   B: 我这个人从来不挑不拣，干什么都可以。

   A: 你要是不挑工作，工作机会就很多。你暑期准备干多长时间？

   B: 我想从五月 15 号起一直干到八月底。

2. Looking for Jobs

   A: 你弟弟找工作找得怎么样了？

   B: 他说现在好的工作都已经被人占了。

   A: 不会吧。其实，我看现在网上有不少工作广告。他去查了没有？

   B: 他说他从一月起就开始在网上找，到现在还没找到个合适的工作。

   A: 报纸上也有不少广告。我们学校的布告栏，他也可以去看看。

   B: 我说话他不听。你跟他说说吧。

   A: 好啊。你放心，你弟弟工作的事儿由我负责，我一定帮他找到一个满意的工作。

   B: 你真够朋友。

TASK 4. PICTURE DESCRIPTION

Describe the pictures using the grammar and the vocabulary you learned in this lesson. Use your imagination!

 读写练习(Dú Xiě Liànxí)
Reading/Writing Exercises

 ## TASK 1. ANALYTICAL READING

Read the following passage and choose the correct words from the choices below to fill in the missing parts. Be careful! Some words may be grammatically correct but not contextually appropriate for a given location.

我的同学张子倩很喜欢看中国电视连续剧。她非常希望中国连续剧能被翻译(1)英文，介绍到美国去。我刚认识她的时候，以为她是搞中国电影的，(2)她是学电脑的。我们还在美国的时候，她就知道很多中国演员和中国明星的名字。谁演过什么电影，电视剧，演得怎么样，她都知道得(3)。这次来中国以前，她跟我说她想来研究中国电影。她还说她想在中国的电影公司里找一(4)工作。昨天她给我来电话，说她找到了。是跟一个导演去拍电视剧。剧里边有几个演员要说些英文，但是他们英文都不好。所以，导演要找一个会说英文，也会说中文的人。张子倩说她(5)三月起，就开始找工作了。她(6)网上、报上的招聘(7)都看了，都没有她想找的工作。后来，她认识的一位朋友告诉她有一个导演正在招聘人，让她赶块去申请。她想这种工作要是登在网上或者报纸上，一定早就(8)人占了。子倩这次运气太好了。昨天她去跟那个负责招聘的人谈了以后，马上就(9)聘用了。而且英文组的事也都(10)她负责。

Supplementary Vocabulary

1. 连续剧	liánxùjù	*n.*	TV series
2. 演员	yǎnyuán	*n.*	actor, actress
演		*v.*	to perform
3. 导演	dǎoyǎn	*n.*	movie director
4. 拍(电影)	pāi	*v.*	to shoot (a film)
5. 登	dēng	*v.*	to be published in…
6. 运气	yùnqi	*n.*	luck

Answer Choices

1. a) 到   b) 作   c) 成   d) 去
2. a) 其实   b) 而且   c) 以为   d) 所以
3. a) 清楚   b) 清清楚楚   c) 太多   d) 多多
4. a) 份   b) 件   c) 分   d) 位
5. a) 从   b) 到   c) 在   d) 开始
6. a) 把   b) 让   c) 由   d) 被
7. a) 人员   b) 广告   c) 工作   d) 演员
8. a) 由   b) 把   c) 叫   d) 聘
9. a) 被   b) 把   c) 让   d) 由
10. a) 由   b) 把   c) 让   d) 被

📖 TASK 2. CHENGYU STORY

Read the 成语故事 below and answer the following questions.

叶公好龙

古代的时候，有一个叫叶子高的人，大家都叫他叶公。叶公非常喜欢龙。他的房子里边到处都画着龙，他的东西上边也画着龙，还用各种材料做了很多龙。有一天，天上的真龙知道了叶公特别喜欢龙，非常高兴，决定找时间去看一下儿叶公。

一天晚上，外边下着大雨，还刮着大风，真龙来到了叶公的家。真龙把头放在叶公家的窗户上，把自己的尾巴放在客厅里面。叶公那时候还没有睡着觉，看见真龙来到了自己的家，吓得要命。衣服都没来得及穿，拔腿就跑走了。

真龙看见叶公吓得那个样子，才知道叶公不是真的喜欢自己，只是喜欢自己的画，或者像自己一样的东西。

Supplementary Vocabulary

1. 叶公好龙	Yègōng hào lóng	*phr.*	(lit.) Mr. Ye is fond of dragons; to pretend to like whatone really fears or dislikes, profess to want revolution but actually fear it
叶		*n.*	a last name
公		*n.*	male
好		*v.*	to like
龙		*n.*	dragon
2. 材料	cáiliào	*n.*	materials
3. 尾巴	wěiba	*n.*	tail

Questions

1. 用自己的话来说一说叶公好龙是什么意思？
2. 你觉得这个故事真正的意思是什么？
3. 你认识象叶公这样的人吗？请你讲一讲这个人的故事。

TASK 3. AUTHENTIC MATERIAL

In this section, you will be exposed to some authentic materials that people use in China. Read the following advertisement for a job and answer the questions.

Questions

1. 哪個單位在找人？
2. 那個單位要找人做什麼工作？
3. 这个工作是不是只要有经验的人？
4. 你对这个工作有没有兴趣？

 TASK 4. E-MAIL

You just started working at a summer job and are eager to tell your friends all about it. Write an e-mail telling your friends where you are working, and whether you like it or not. How many hours a week do you work? Do you like working there? What kinds of things are you doing there? Be sure to use the grammar and vocabulary from this lesson!

39
用手机
Using Cell Phones

 听力练习 (Tīnglì Liànxí)
Listening Exercises

 TASK 1. BINGO

In this section, you will hear various Chinese phrases and sentences. Demonstrate your understanding of them by numbering their English counterparts in the order in which you hear them.

A. Phrases

public pay phone

generous or stingy

to decide to open a cell phone account

incoming message display function

to pay deposit

to waste time

free local phone calls within the city

very attractive

monthly charge and usage fee

international long distance

to send a short message

to discover problems

time to be off duty

school campus

to find out something informally

to end the sales promotion

B. Sentences

Your cell phone works only if you put in the deposit.

He didn't buy his cell phone to be fashionable, but rather for the sake of convenience.

Besides a display for incoming messages, my cell phone can also send short text messages.

I don't feel like using public phones all the time. Let's go to the sales division of the telecommunications bureau and buy a cell phone.

I was originally planning to open a cell phone account for him. But I discovered afterwards that using cell phones is very expensive.

If you use your cell phone to make international calls, you are too extravagant.

It is not going to be expensive if there are free minutes included.

In addition to him, I am also very generous.

The promotion ends today when everyone goes off duty.

🎧💻 TASK 2. SHORT CONVERSATIONS

Listen to the short conversations. Select the correct answer for each question from the choices provided.

1. 能/不能
2. 有/没有
3. 有/没有
4. 要/不要

🎧💻 TASK 3. MONOLOGUE

Listen to the two passages and answer the questions below.

Passage 1

1. What is the speaker talking about?

   a) The speaker wants to buy a cell phone.

   b) The speaker wants to sell a cell phone.

   c) The speaker wants to upgrade his cell phone.

   d) None of the above.

2. Which of the following statements is NOT correct?

   a) The man can help open a cell phone account.

   b) The man is very proud of his cell phones.

   c) The man has opened a cell phone account for himself.

   d) None of the above.

Passage 2

1. What is the speaker talking about?

   a) She has bought a cell phone and still has lots of money left.

   b) She wants to buy a cell phone but does not have enough money.

   c) She has bought a cell phone, and now she has no money left.

   d) None of the above.

2. Which of the following statements is NOT correct?

    a) The store where the speaker bought her cell phone is very busy.

    b) The store only sells small, trendy cell phones.

    c) The cell phone the woman purchased was not very expensive.

    d) All of the above.

🎧💻 TASK 4. DIALOGUE

Listen to the dialogue and answer the questions below.

1. What is the conversation about?

    a) The woman wants to get a cell phone.

    b) The man wants to get a cell phone.

    c) The woman does not want to get a cell phone.

    d) The man does not want to get a cell phone.

2. Which one of the following is NOT correct?

    a) The man is satisfied with his cell phone.

    b) The woman does not like the man's cell phone.

    c) The woman is trendy.

    d) All of the above.

3. What is the relationship between the man and the woman?

    a) a salesperson and a customer

    b) two salespeople

    c) two customers

    d) two friends

4. Which of the following statements is correct?

    a) The man does not want the woman to use his cell phone.

    b) The woman does not want the man to use her cell phone.

    c) The man's cell phone does not work.

    d) The woman's cell phone does not work.

口语练习(Kǒuyǔ Liànxí)
Speaking Exercises

 TASK 1. SUBSTITUTION

Familiarize yourself with basic sentence patterns by substituting the given phrases into the following sentences.

1. A: 你们除了(手机开户)以外，还(谈)到了什么？

   B: 我们还(谈)到了(手机的座机费)。

银行的手续	谈	银行的利息
那件衣服	找	一条裤子
成语故事	学	中国文化
电子邮件	收	一封信
语法书	买	一本词典

2. A: 除了他以外，你们谁还(有手机)？

   B: 我们都(用公用电话)。

带现金	带旅行支票
坐地铁去	乘公共汽车去
说明天是晴天	觉得明天要下雨
被大使馆拒签了	拿到签证了

3. A: 有多少人(不想参加促销活动)？

   B: 除了我以外，(还有几个人)也(不想参加促销活动)。

没有带定金	我的室友
不想上电脑补习班	我们班的同学
没有找到临时工作	他们俩

不喜欢游泳   那三个人

不爱讲价钱   我的一些朋友

4. A: 我能不能（在外地用手机）？

   B: 只要你（办了手机升级），就可以（在外地用手机）。

办借记卡   银行帐户里有钱

马上开帐户   存的是银行支票

坐地铁去   熟悉地铁路线

过马路   看见红绿灯是绿色的

上飞机   有登机牌

5. 只有（在市内），你才能（用免费分钟）。

银行收到了钱   开帐户

在外地找到了工作   离开这儿

拿开那张报纸   看见你的支票

开开电视   看到新闻

🎧💻 TASK 2. QUICK RESPONSE

The following exercise will challenge your listening and speaking abilities and help you to develop good conversational skills.

A. Answering Questions

Listen to the following questions and provide an answer to each one. If you don't know a word, try to guess its meaning from the context, rather than looking it up. Remember, both speed and accuracy are important!

1. 入网是什么意思？

2. 你喜欢不喜欢用手机？为什么？

3. 你觉得手机的哪些功能最有用？

4. 你觉得在中国办手机开户容易吗？为什么？

B. Asking Questions

Listen to the following statements and follow the hints in the right-hand column to ask a related question for each statement. Try to avoid using the 吗-type question.

		Hints
1.	我买手机不是赶时髦，是图方便。	（是不是）
2.	我的手机有来电显示，还能发短信息。	（哪些）
3.	他的手机是免费的。	（多少钱）
4.	这个活动今天下班的时候就结束了。	（什么时候）

🎧💻 TASK 3. GUIDED ROLE-PLAYING

Listen to the following dialogues between two native speakers. Then select Role A or Role B and have a dialogue with the computer. After familiarizing yourself with the conversation, construct and record your own dialogue by replacing as many words as possible with related terms. Be creative, but be careful not to disrupt the structure of the conversation!

1. Opening a Cell Phone Account

   A: 我想办入网手续。那种手机多少钱？

   B: 三百五十块一个。

   A: 你们现在最便宜的卡有没有免费分钟？

   B: 没有。打一分钟交一分钟的钱，但是接电话不要钱。

   A: 我要是去外地几天，我的手机还能用吗？

   B: 能用。但是你要办手机升级，还要交漫游费。

2. Discussing the Advantages and Disadvantages of Using Cell Phones

   A: 手机太贵，不值得。我下个月不想用手机了。

   B: 为什么？你不是说你每个月的座机费不高吗？

   A: 是啊。但是使用费太高了。

   B: 你少用一点儿，使用费就不会那么高了。

   A: 唉，虽然我不用，可是别人还是要用。我现在每天要接几十个电话。

   B: 那你为什么不换那种接电话不要钱的卡呢？

   A: 那种卡的座机费要比我现在这种卡高。

TASK 4. PICTURE DESCRIPTION

Describe the pictures using the grammar and the vocabulary you learned in this lesson. Use your imagination!

 读写练习(Dú Xiě Liànxí)

Reading/Writing Exercises

 TASK 1. SHORT STORY

Read the story and answer the questions that follow.

我们也有手机

一天，阿乐的太太下班以后，带回家了一个公司发给她的手机。那个手机不但有来电显示，而且还能发短信息。阿乐看见以后非常喜欢，他也到电信局给自己开了个手机帐户，买了个很时髦的手机。他为了炫耀他和他太太的手机，就决定请阿笑和阿笑的太太这个周末到饭馆去吃饭。

星期天中午，四个人到饭馆刚刚坐好，没有说上几句话阿乐的手机就响了，过了一会儿，阿乐的太太的手机也响了，他们俩怕阿笑和阿笑的太太没有注意到他们的手机，所以就开始大声地说话。而且，声音越来越大。过了好一会儿，阿笑对阿乐说，饭馆里很多人都在看着你和你太太打电话。阿乐得意地说："没事儿，我这不是私人谈话，不怕别人听见。"阿笑说："我知道，你们是想炫耀你们的手机，所以才请我们吃饭。我和我太太今天虽然没有带我们的手机，但是我们也都有手机了。你们不要再打电话了。我们吃饭吧。阿乐问阿笑："你怎么知道我们在炫耀我们的手机？"阿笑回答说："我几个月前买了手机后，也干过你们这种事，后来使用费太高了，就不再炫耀了！"

Supplementary Vocabulary

1. 炫耀　　　xuànyào　　　v.　　　to show off
2. 响　　　　xiǎng　　　　v.　　　to sound
3. 得意　　　déyì　　　　adj.　　　complacent, self-satisfied
4. 私人　　　sīrén　　　　adj.　　　private

Questions

1. 阿乐和他太太为什么请阿笑和阿笑的太太去饭馆吃饭？
   a) 因为他们很久没见面了。
   b) 因为他们想让阿笑知道他们有手机了。
   c) 因为他们想知道阿笑有没有手机？
   d) a) + b) + c) 都不对。
2. 阿乐为什么去买了个手机？
   a) 因为他太太叫他买个手机。
   b) 因为他喜欢阿笑的手机。
   c) 因为他喜欢阿乐太太的手机。
   d) a) + b) + c) 都不对。

3. 阿笑和他太太为什么不炫耀他们的手机？

   a) 因为他们不想让别人知道他们有手机。

   b) 因为他们怕花钱。

   c) 因为他们的手机坏了。

   d) a) + b) + c) 都不对。

4. 谁最先买的手机？

   a) 阿笑和他太太

   b) 阿乐和他太太

   c) 阿乐的太太

   d) a) + b) + c) 都不对

 TASK 2. CHENGYU STORY

Read the 成语故事 below and answer the following questions.

对牛弹琴

古代的时候，有一个人，弹琴弹得可好听了。每次他弹琴的时候，很多人听到他的琴声，就会停下来，一动也不动地听他弹琴。有一次，那个弹琴的人到一个很远很远的地方去游玩。一天早上，他站在一个小山坡上，往远一看，蓝蓝的天，白白的云，绿绿的草地，草地上还有几头牛在吃草。那个弹琴的人看见这么漂亮的风景的时候，就想起来了一个动物跟着音乐跳舞的故事。他想动物也懂音乐，这些动物在这么漂亮的地方不跳舞是不是因为这儿没有音乐呢？所以，他就拿出自己的琴，坐在山坡上认认真真地弹起琴来。他的琴声虽然很好听，可是那几头牛好像没有听见一样，还是在草地上慢慢地吃草。这个弹琴的人非常生气，他想"是不是我的琴弹得不好，这些牛才不跟着我的琴声跳舞呢？他气得吃不下饭，睡不着觉。后来，他的一个好心的朋友告诉他说："这些牛不跟着你的琴声跳舞，不是因为你琴弹得不好，只是那些牛不懂琴声。"

Supplementary Vocabulary

1. 对牛弹琴	duì niú tán qín	*phr.*	(lit.) to play a musical instrument to a cow; waste one's time, talk to the wall, preach to deaf ears
牛		*n.*	ox, cow
弹琴		*v. obj.*	to play a musical instrument
2. 古	gǔ	*adj.*	ancient
3. 一动也不动	yīdòng yě bùdòng	*phr.*	not making a single move, standing still
4. 山坡	shānpō	*n.*	hill

Questions

1. 用自己的话讲一讲对牛弹琴是什么意思？

2. 这个弹琴的人为什么生气？你觉得他应该不应该生气？为什么？

3. 你或者你朋友有没有对牛弹琴的经历？请讲讲这些经历。

🖥 TASK 3. AUTHENTIC MATERIAL

If you want to open a cell phone account in China, you need to fill out an application form. Here is a form used by one company in China. Challenge yourself and see if you are able to answer the questions that follow and then you complete the form.

Questions

1. 这是一个什么广告？
2. 这个广告有几种服务项目？
3. 广告单上，什么服务项目的费用是一样的？
4. 在广告单上，有没有免费的服务项目？

 ## TASK 4. E-MAIL

You have just opened a cell phone account in China, and you are eager to share the experience with your friends back home. Write them an e-mail to tell them about it. Why did you want to open the account? What are the procedures for opening an account, and how do you make monthly payments? What features does your cell phone have? Can you call long distance or overseas? Why or why not?

40

汉语水平考试
Taking the HSK

 听力练习 (Tīnglì Liànxí)
Listening Exercises

 TASK 1. BINGO

In this section, you will hear various Chinese phrases and sentences. Demonstrate your understanding of them by numbering their English counterparts in the order in which you hear them.

A. Phrases

(I) may flunk a test	oral expression
to obtain a government certification	to never get anxious
does not care at all	basic portion
main tasks	test content
comprehensive knowledge	a paragraph of dialogue
test paper of simulated tests	listening and reading comprehension
fill in the blanks	grammar structure
to feel like you are gaining (learning) something	to check each other's homework

B. Sentences

He feels that the grammar structures are becoming more and more difficult to learn.

If he does not preview the lessons before class, he will not be able to understand them.

Everyone who wants to work or study in China should take the Chinese Proficiency Test.

It looks like it is easy to flunk the exam if you are careless.

I did not understand that section of the dialogue, so when I took the test I was very flustered.

Although his mother tongue is not Chinese, he does specialized Chinese research.

My roommate does not care about his grades. He does not even read his textbooks before exams.

He never spends time working especially on his listening skills, but his listening comprehension is very good.

I feel that we should review comprehensive fill-in-the-blank exercises; maybe tomorrow's test will have this item.

🎧💻 TASK 2. SHORT CONVERSATIONS

Listen to the short conversations. Select the correct answer for each question from the choices provided.

1. 很好/不好
2. 应该/不应该
3. 复习完了/没复习完
4. 难/不难

🎧💻 TASK 3. MONOLOGUE

Listen to the two passages and answer the questions below.

Passage 1

1. What is this woman talking about?

   a) She is very good at taking tests.

   b) She does not take tests well.

   c) She does not understand the material.

   d) None of the above.

2. Which of the following is correct?

   a) The woman does not study at all.

   b) The woman does all her practice exercises.

   c) The woman does not do practice exercises.

   d) None of the above.

Passage 2

1. What is this man talking about?

   a) He does not understand how his friend studies.

   b) He always studies by himself.

   c) He is satisfied with the progress he is making.

   d) All of the above.

2. Which of the following is correct?

   a) The more the man studies, the more confident he becomes.

   b) The man has to listen to music while studying.

   c) The man's friend listens to music while studying.

   d) None of the above.

🎧💻 TASK 4. DIALOGUE

Listen to the dialogue and answer the questions below.

1. What are the two speakers talking about?

   a) how to improve their reading skills

   b) how to improve their listening skills

   c) how to do better on an exam

   d) all of the above

2. When does this conversation take place?

   a) after they do reading and listening exercises

   b) before they do reading and listening exercises

   c) after their exam

   d) before their exam

3. Which of the following is correct?

   a) The man did very well on the listening and reading part of the exam.

   b) The man did not do well on the listening and reading part of the exam.

   c) The man did very well on the listening but not the reading part of the exam.

   d) The man did very well on the reading but not the listening part of the exam.

4. Which of the following is NOT correct?

   a) The man has a larger vocabulary.

   b) The man reads more than the woman.

   c) The two speakers intend to study together.

   d) All of the above.

口语练习 (Kǒuyǔ Liànxí)
Speaking Exercises

 TASK 1. SUBSTITUTION

Familiarize yourself with basic sentence patterns by substituting the given phrases into the following sentences.

1. 连（我）都（认识这个字）。

他	会跳舞
我弟弟	能发电子邮件
我奶奶	在学英文

2. 他连（一个朋友）也（没有）。

一分钱	不愿意花
一分钟的时间	不肯等
一句话	说不出来

3. 他连（吃）也没（吃），就（走）了。

试	买
问	拿走
看	坐下去
听	离开
想	跑进去

4. 他（累）得连（饭）都忘了（吃）。

急	衣服	换
忙	水	喝
慌	名字	写

5. 他连(星期天)都(在图书馆学习)。

    夏天　　　　　　　　要出去跑步

    冬天　　　　　　　　开着空调

    上课的时候　　　　　睡觉

    周末　　　　　　　　不肯休息

6. 他连在(图书馆)都(会大声说话)。

    车里　　　　　　　　要听音乐

    自己的家　　　　　　睡不好觉

    工作单位　　　　　　不听话

    学校　　　　　　　　不学习

7. 凡是(参加汉语水平考试)的人都(能得到证书)。

    逛过夜市　　　　　　知道小贩很油

    去过那家饭馆　　　　会再去

    暑期打工　　　　　　能挣到一些零花钱

    得流感　　　　　　　会发烧

    有手机　　　　　　　不愿意用公用电话

8. 我们越(吃)越(爱吃)。

    学　　　　　　　　　糊涂

    累　　　　　　　　　应该锻炼

    听音乐　　　　　　　想听

    看时间　　　　　　　着急

9. 他越(卖关子)，我越(好奇)。

    问我　　　　　　　　心慌

    夸我　　　　　　　　不好意思

    跟我诉苦　　　　　　不想帮他

    要我学习　　　　　　想去看电影

🎧💻 TASK 2. QUICK RESPONSE

The following exercise will challenge your listening and speaking abilities and help you to develop good conversational skills.

A. Answering Questions

Listen to the following questions and provide an answer to each one. If you don't know a word, try to guess its meaning from the context, rather than looking it up. Remember, both speed and accuracy are important!

1. 你想不想去参加汉语水平考试，为什么？

2. 你觉得考试的前一天应不应该学习？为什么？

3. 你觉得看中文电影是不是准备听力考试的好办法，为什么？

4. 汉语水平考试都考些什么内容？

B. Asking Questions

Listen to the following statements and follow the hints in the right-hand column to ask a related question for each statement. Try to avoid using the 吗-type question.

                                                     Hints

1. 我去年参加汉语水平考试以后，得到了一个二级证书。   （什么）

2. 汉语水平考试的对象是那些母语不是中文的人。   （谁）

3. 中国的汉语水平考试一共有十一级。   （多少级）

4. 我们连星期五晚上都做综合填空题和练习写作。   （星期几）

🎧💻 TASK 3. GUIDED ROLE-PLAYING

Listen to the following dialogues between two native speakers. Select Role A or Role B and have a dialogue with the computer. After familiarizing yourself with the conversation, construct and record your own dialogue by replacing as many words as possible with related terms. Be creative, but be careful not to disrupt the structure of the conversation!

1. What is the HSK?

   A: 你知道什么是 HSK 吗？

   B: HSK 是汉语水平考试的简称。我听说今年十月份有汉语水平考试，你想考吗？

   A: 不知道。考汉语水平考试有什么用？

   B: 你可以申请去中国大学学中文的奖学金。

   A: 真的。有这么好的事儿？能在中国学习多长时间？

   B: 一年、一个学期、或暑期一个月，等等。汉语水平考试有基础，初中等和高等三套试卷。怎么样？你跟我一起考初中等吧。

   A: 我才学了两年的中文，我还是考基础吧。

2. Let's Study Together for the HSK

   A: 今年十月我想参加基础的汉语水平考试，看看我能考几级。

   B: 我想考初中等。我们一块儿复习吧。

   A: 我听说汉语水平考试考的是汉语水平的综合知识，挺难的。

   B: 说难也难，说不难也不难。听力理解和阅读理解，平时多听，多读就行了。

   A: 语法结构和综合填空呢？我们怎么复习？

   B: 我们得好好地把语法过一遍，然后再把模拟题做几遍，就行了。当然练习题做得越多越好。

   A: 好，我听你的。咱们今天晚上就开始复习吧。

TASK 4. PICTURE DESCRIPTION

Describe the pictures using the grammar and the vocabulary you learned in this lesson. Use your imagination!

 读写练习(Dú Xiě Liànxí)
Reading/Writing Exercises

💻 TASK 1. COMPREHENSIVE READING

Read the following passage and fill in the blanks. Then answer the true/false questions that follow.

我去年考了一次汉语水平考试。考试的前一个月，我定了一个复习计划。_____是老师讲的生词和语法我都复习了。考试的那天，我_____本就不紧张。可是那天考完试以后我才知道，汉语水平考试跟老师给我们的考试不一样，是一种标准_____的考试。比老师给我们的难多了，词汇量也大多了。听_____和阅_____那两项很多我根本就不懂。填_____那一项以前我也从来都没有见过。那天我考完以后，觉得很难过。我以_____我的汉语已经学得很好了，没想到还有那么多东西我都不会。后来我去找我的中文老师谈了一次。老师说：你怎么_____来都没告诉过我你要去参加汉语水平考试？我说：我想等到考完了，拿到_____书了，再告诉你，给你一个惊喜。根本没想到会考糊。老师笑着说：别难过。我借给你一本汉语水平模拟考题。你做了一定会有收_____。她借给我的那本书真有用。_____来我自己又买了几本，认认_____地复习了一年。凡是书上的题，像语法结_____和综合知_____填空等我都做了。我今年十月份又参加了一次 HSK 考试。那天可比第一_____考试心_____多了。考完以后，我还想：说不定这次又考糊了。过了一段时间，考试中心给我寄来了一份中国政_____发的汉 语水_____证书。我高兴得要命，因为我考了个四级。我现在越学中文_____想学，我明年说不定还能考_____六级呢。

Supplementary Vocabulary

1. 惊喜　　　　jīngxǐ　　　　*n.*　　　　surprise
2. 难过　　　　nánguò　　　　*adj.*　　　　sad, feeling bad
3. 考试中心　　kǎoshì zhōngxīn　*n. phr.*　　testing center

Questions

1. 汉语水平考试我一共考了三次。　　　　　　　　　　True/False
2. 第一次我连汉语水平考试考什么都不知道，就去考了。　True/False
3. 第二次考试的题目，有两项我都考糊了。　　　　　　True/False
4. 我越考越有自信心，越不紧张。　　　　　　　　　　True/False

 TASK 2. CHENGYU STORY

Read the 成语故事 below and answer the following questions.

一举两得

古代的时候，有一个非常勇敢的人，他什么都不害怕。有一天，他和他的一个朋友在路上，看见两只老虎，一大一小，正在吃马肉。他马上要过去把两只老虎杀了。他的朋友说，你别着急。你一个人打两只老虎很危险。你应该耐心地在这儿等一会儿再过去。这个年轻人不理解他朋友的意思，就问他朋友说，我现在过去和等一会儿再过去有什么不一样？

他的朋友回答说：你看那两只老虎吃得那么香，一会儿吃完了肉，肯定会打起来，小老虎会被大老虎打死，大老虎也会很累，你那会儿再过去打老虎，就可以一举两得了。

那个人觉得自己的朋友说得很对。就在路边耐心地等着。过了一会儿，两只老虎真的打了起来，小老虎被大老虎打死了，大老虎也累得不行了。这时候，那个年轻人上去很快就把大老虎杀死了。

Supplementary Vocabulary

1.	一举两得	yī jǔ liǎng dé	*phr.*	to kill two birds with one stone, dual gain
	举		*n.*	an action
	得		*v.*	to obtain
2.	古代	gǔdài	*n.*	ancient times
3.	勇敢	yǒnggǎn	*adj.*	brave
4.	老虎	lǎohǔ	*n.*	tiger
5.	马肉	mǎròu	*n.*	horse's meat
6.	杀	shā	*v.*	to kill
7.	危险	wēixiǎn	*adj.*	dangerous

Questions

1. 在这个故事里，"一举"代表什么？"两得"呢？
2. 你能不能讲几个"一举两得"的故事？

⬛ TASK 3. AUTHENTIC MATERIAL

In this section, you will be exposed to authentic materials used for HSK test. Complete the form. Then challenge yourself and see if you are able to answer the questions that follow.

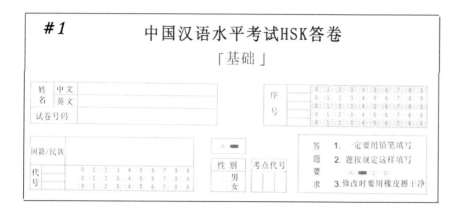

1. 如果你要参加 HSK 的口试，应该填哪一张表？
2. 如果你学汉语的时间不长，应该不应该参加 HSK 口试？
3. 如果你只学了一个学期的汉语，现在要考 HSK，应该填哪张表？
4. 如果你已经学了一、两年的中文了，现在要考 HSK，应该填哪张表？

💻 TASK 4. WEB SURFING

Go to **http://www.hsk.org.cn** and see if you can find some information on HSK testing. In Chinese, write a brief summary of your findings and e-mail it to your professor.